New Frontiers in Regional Science: Asian Perspectives

Volume 83

This series is a constellation of works by scholars in the field of regional science and in related disciplines specifically focusing on dynamism in Asia.

Asia is the most dynamic part of the world. Japan, Korea, Taiwan, and Singapore experienced rapid and miracle economic growth in the 1970s. Malaysia, Indonesia, and Thailand followed in the 1980s. China, India, and Vietnam are now rising countries in Asia and are even leading the world economy. Due to their rapid economic development and growth, Asian countries continue to face a variety of urgent issues including regional and institutional unbalanced growth, environmental problems, poverty amidst prosperity, an ageing society, the collapse of the bubble economy, and deflation, among others.

Asian countries are diversified as they have their own cultural, historical, and geographical as well as political conditions. Due to this fact, scholars specializing in regional science as an inter- and multi-discipline have taken leading roles in providing mitigating policy proposals based on robust interdisciplinary analysis of multifaceted regional issues and subjects in Asia. This series not only will present unique research results from Asia that are unfamiliar in other parts of the world because of language barriers, but also will publish advanced research results from those regions that have focused on regional and urban issues in Asia from different perspectives.

The series aims to expand the frontiers of regional science through diffusion of intrinsically developed and advanced modern regional science methodologies in Asia and other areas of the world. Readers will be inspired to realize that regional and urban issues in the world are so vast that their established methodologies still have space for development and refinement, and to understand the importance of the interdisciplinary and multidisciplinary approach that is inherent in regional science for analyzing and resolving urgent regional and urban issues in Asia.

Topics under consideration in this series include the theory of social cost and benefit analysis and criteria of public investments, socio-economic vulnerability against disasters, food security and policy, agro-food systems in China, industrial clustering in Asia, comprehensive management of water environment and resources in a river basin, the international trade bloc and food security, migration and labor market in Asia, land policy and local property tax, Information and Communication Technology planning, consumer "shop-around" movements, and regeneration of downtowns, among others.

Researchers who are interested in publishing their books in this Series should obtain a proposal form from Yoshiro Higano (Editor in Chief, higano@jsrsai.jp) and return the completed form to him.

Keiko Nosse Hirono • Kazuhiro Yaguchi
Editors

Reconstruction Period and the Stages of Regeneration After a Great Earthquake

Experience from the Great East Japan Earthquake

Springer

Editors
Keiko Nosse Hirono
College of Economics
Nihon University
Chiyoda-ku, Tokyo, Japan

Kazuhiro Yaguchi
Faculty of Economics
Keiai University
Chiba-shi, Chiba, Japan

ISSN 2199-5974 ISSN 2199-5982 (electronic)
New Frontiers in Regional Science: Asian Perspectives
ISBN 978-981-96-8821-0 ISBN 978-981-96-8822-7 (eBook)
https://doi.org/10.1007/978-981-96-8822-7

This Springer imprint is published by the registered company Springer Nature Singapore Pte Ltd.
The registered company address is: 152 Beach Road, #21-01/04 Gateway East, Singapore 189721, Singapore

Preface

This book is possibly the first of its kind to propose concrete ideas and suggestions for reconstruction and creation of a region in the aftermath of a massive earthquake. The contents are drawn by the authors of each chapter based on their analyses and experiences of the Great East Japan Earthquake. The book offers analyses of the reconstruction period and the stages of regeneration after the earthquake from many perspectives: economy, mental health, social business, interregional risk-sharing system, city planning, housing, and industrial revival. The authors also attempt to address the existing problems in Tohoku Area 14 years after the Great East Japan Earthquake; the problems are both hardware—for example, city reconstruction, housing, and industrial regeneration—and software—mental health care and quality of life (QoL) of the people in the region.

Reconstructing the Tohoku region involves (1) retaining skilled employees to engage in projects and business to reconstruct the region, and resolving the manpower issue caused by the outflow of the working-age population; (2) alleviating shortage of firms' business funding, inhabitants' living funds, and local governments' financial resources; (3) creating demand for the goods and services produced in the Tohoku region; (4) city planning for safety and efficiency; (5) earthquake-proof conversion of housing for safety; (6) reconstructing the community by social business; (7) implementing measures to curb alcohol dependence after the Great East Japan Earthquake; and (8) risk-sharing of natural disaster among the regions.

Analyzing these elements in detail, first, the cost of reconstruction of capital stock after the disaster has to be restricted. For reconstruction, we require stable securement of human resources and measures to control prices of materials. Second, we have to ensure sustainable development of the economy after the earthquake, especially since the Tohoku region faces several serious problems, such as outflow of human resources owing to a lack of employment opportunities, an aging population, and the financial difficulties of the local governments worsened by the Great East Japan Earthquake. Third, restoration assistance following the earthquake must be considered, specifically, in terms of subsidies and loans of business funds, and livelihood support for the needy. The aforementioned serious issues must be resolved and new industries developed to ensure successive demand for the goods and services emerging from the Tohoku region by utilizing its potential and by providing financial support.

With realization of new investment in disaster prevention, recovery, and reconstruction after the Great East Japan Earthquake, we felt a necessity to study interregional risk-sharing through public insurance as well as investment in disaster prevention, recovery, and reconstruction. In Japan, system design with the concept of risk-sharing of natural disasters among regions is important for the whole country from the standpoint of efficiency, because of the high risk of natural disasters.

Social business also plays an important role in developing communities in the affected areas through job creation, thus leading to an increment in the population. Population growth raises consumption, which, in turn, revitalizes the regional economy. Therefore, the issues for the promotion of social business should be examined.

To secure the lives of inhabitants, houses have to be made earthquake-proof, especially rental houses where earthquake-proof conversion has not progressed smoothly. Profitability is an important point to consider when making houses earthquake-proof, because the process of conversion of housing is expensive, requiring enough rental income compared to the cost of the conversion. If earthquake-proof conversion of housing is not profitable, a policy must be drafted and implemented to complement the lack of profitability and accelerate earthquake-proof conversion of housing.

The severe stress, sense of loss, and lack of a place to call home caused by the unprecedented disaster of the Great East Japan Earthquake led some people of the Tohoku region to become alcohol-dependent. Therefore, it is important to take measures against alcohol-related problems as well in the affected areas.

Therefore, in this book, first, we include research results from the economic analyses of the Great East Japan. Second, we present methods and models to analyze in economics the way to reconstruct and regenerate the devastated area. Third, we propose directions for policies that can resolve the aforementioned problems, reflecting the needs of residents, and that give merits to local governments. Fourth, economists and welfare psychologists (including a mental health social worker), who are closely related to the devastated area, propose policies from perspectives that emphasize the field and are in line with the reality of the area. Fifth, a city planning policy based on efficiency, disaster prevention, and convenience of the aged inhabitants, considering compact city policies and public transportation, is proposed. Sixth, we provide methods for making earthquake-proof construction work profitable for rental firms and accelerate earthquake-proof conversion of housing using local governments' financial support. We also make a theoretical and practical comparison to understand whether tax reduction or subsidy is superior for promoting earthquake-proof conversion of rental housing.

Seventh, we propose ways of doing successful social business and identify the possible problems within them in order to resolve social issues. Social business can bring about increment in work place and thus population, and demand for goods and services.

Eighth, we propose a method to solve the alcohol-related problems of the affected area devastated by the earthquake and a way of providing a support network for them and for supporters to overcome sufferer's addiction several years after the Great East Japan Earthquake.

Ninth, we develop a spatial computable general equilibrium (SCGE) model to measure the damage caused by the Great East Japan Earthquake and the effects of reconstruction investment and public investment, and theoretically examine a fiscal system for interregional risk-sharing against natural disasters.

In Chap. 2, we present a collective impact social business that is undertaken through public and private agents and that can resolve regional issues and co-create regional communities through entrepreneurship in the affected areas. We also identify several problems of the social business.

In Chap. 3, we explore urban development and town planning in the Tohoku region after the Great East Japan Earthquake, underscoring the need for a compact city with relatively high residential density. With a high aging rate (over 65) and ongoing depopulation, a compact city around the safe city center would be ideal to improve and maintain social infrastructure efficiently from a financial viewpoint. Regional development based on the concept of a compact city is not only efficient but also safe in terms of movement from the coastal area, with its risk of tsunami disasters, to the city center. Simultaneously, a public transportation policy is proposed for improving the mobility of the aging population in the affected area.

In Chap. 4, we present the contents of interviews conducted with supporters and members of a self-help group, who realized changes in local responses to alcohol-related problems because of their various efforts. However, based on the interviews, we suggest a method to build a supporting network in the vast, aged, disaster-struck, and depopulated region.

In Chap. 5, we estimate consumers' willingness to pay for earthquake-proof conversions of rental apartments and construct a model to compute rental firms' profits from earthquake-proof conversions of rental apartments. Using the model of rental firms' profits, we develop a framework to determine the need for and amount of financial support from the local government and compare tax breaks and subsidies as methods of financial support. Empirical estimates are calculated in Tokyo and the affected area.

In Chap. 6, we theoretically examine interregional risk-sharing through public insurance as well as investment in disaster prevention, recovery, and reconstruction. An SCGE analysis is conducted to quantitatively demonstrate the asymmetric spillover effects of the earthquake and reconstruction investment and clarify the extent to which public insurance improves welfare.

Overall, several new methods of analyses useful for research are proposed, for example, a method to estimate (a) whether companies can earn profits from the earthquake-proof conversion of rental houses and (b) the amount of financial support necessary for the earthquake-proof conversion of housing (Chap. 5). Further, an SCGE model is proposed, in which a decrease in regional income through investment in disaster prevention, recovery, and reconstruction is endogenous (Chap. 6).

Most of the authors of this book worked at the university in Tohoku Area at the time of the Great East Japan Earthquake, conducted their research in Tohoku Area, or were born in Tohoku Area; thus, they have firsthand knowledge of the area and the influence of the Great East Japan Earthquake. Therefore, the recommendations made in this book are concrete, realistic, and solution-oriented.

The challenges faced by the Tohoku region after the Great East Japan Earthquake—population aging, lack of human resources, decrease in demand for goods and services, mental disorders, and natural disaster—are the same that could be faced by Japan as well as many other countries worldwide in the near future. Therefore, we hope the contents of this book provide hints to solve future problems.

Tokyo, Japan Keiko Nosse Hirono
Chiba, Japan Kazuhiro Yaguchi

Acknowledgments

We are grateful to Professor Akira Yokoyama, the president of Japan College of Social Work, for his support for the authors and helpful comments at academic conferences. We are indebted to the late Professor Naomi Maruo, Keio University, for contributing toward the foundation of this research. We would like to express our gratitude to Mr. Tokuji Ootsuka, Taisei Shuppan, for his valuable advice.

We would like to thank Shinji Otake, Associate Professor, and Masato Takahama, Assistant Professor, both teaching at Tohoku Bunka Gakuen University, for their great cooperation in conducting the survey. We express gratitude to Naohiro Nakagawa, the Representative Director of Public Interest Incorporated Foundation of Japan Challenger Project, and Daisuke Matsui, the President of Oriai Corp., for providing knowledge.

This research was partially supported by the Japanese Government (Ministry of Education, Culture, Sports, Science and Technology), the Grants-in-aid for Scientific Research (C) (JP19K01693 Naoki Sakamoto, JP19K01480 Shumpei Yaoita, JP18K02140 Maiko Wakabayashi).

We are very grateful to Professor Higano, who kindly reviewed the contents of this book as the editor-in-chief of the series *New Frontiers in Regional Science: Asian Perspective*. We are thankful to Mr. Yutaka Hirachi, Ms. Grace James, and Ms. Thirumangai Thamizhmani of Springer for their cooperation.

Contents

List of Contributors

Keiko Nosse Hirono College of Economics, Nihon University, Chiyoda-ku, Tokyo, Japan

Kazunori Nakajima School of Human Science and Environment, University of Hyogo, Hyogo, Japan

Naoki Sakamoto Faculty of Humanities and Social Sciences, Yamagata University, Yamagata, Japan

Maiko Wakabayashi Faculty of Human Welfare, Tokyo Online University, Tokyo, Japan

Kazuhiro Yaguchi Faculty of Economics, Keiai University, Chiba-shi, Chiba, Japan

Shumpei Yaoita College of Regional Development, Shukutoku University, Saitama, Japan

Chapter 1
Earthquake Damage in Japan and Our Contribution

Kazuhiro Yaguchi and Keiko Nosse Hirono

Abstract This book was written in response to the Great East Japan Earthquake that occurred on March 11, 2011. This chapter serves as an introduction to the entire book. The contents of this chapter are, first, the damage caused by the Great East Japan Earthquake and the current status of reconstruction. The damage situation is compared with that of the Great Hanshin-Awaji Earthquake and the 2016 Kumamoto Earthquake. From this, we extract the characteristics of the Great East Japan Earthquake. Second, it outlines the reconstruction plan of the government and Miyagi Prefecture in response to the Great East Japan Earthquake. From these, we point out issues and challenges related to recovery and reconstruction policies. In particular, it points out that recovery and reconstruction policies are similar to the contents of previous regional policies. Third, it outlines and characterizes the five articles included in the book and indicates the contributions of each article.

Keywords Earthquake damage · Great East Japan Earthquake · Recovery plan · Reconstruction policy

K. Yaguchi (✉)
Faculty of Economics, Keiai University, Chiba-shi, Chiba, Japan
e-mail: k-yaguchi@u-keiai.ac.jp

K. N. Hirono
College of Economics, Nihon University, Chiyoda-ku, Tokyo, Japan
e-mail: hirono.keiko@nihon-u.ac.jp

K. N. Hirono, K. Yaguchi (eds.), *Reconstruction Period and the Stages of Regeneration After a Great Earthquake*, New Frontiers in Regional Science: Asian Perspectives 83, https://doi.org/10.1007/978-981-96-8822-7_1

1.1 Introduction

The Great East Japan Earthquake occurred on March 11, 2011. In the aftermath of the earthquake, Japan was faced with the major challenge of restoring and reconstructing the affected areas. In response, the government established the "Reconstruction Design Council in response to the Great East Japan Earthquake" immediately after the disaster. At the end of June 2011, it released a "Toward Reconstruction: Hope beyond the disaster." This proposal outlines a basic vision for reconstruction. It emphasized the government's commitment to not only restoring the affected areas but also using the disaster as an opportunity to build a new regional society. Then, at the end of July 2011, the government announced the "Basic Policies for Reconstruction from the Great East Japan Earthquake," which included specific programs.

The basic policies for reconstruction set forth the time schedule and financial resources for restoration and reconstruction. It also sets forth what is necessary to implement the policy, and then provides specific program details. These are reflected in the recovery plans of the affected municipalities. Affected municipalities formulated their own recovery plans, while taking advantage of regional characteristics. The basic policies for reconstruction set the reconstruction period at 10 years, and the five-year period after the earthquake was positioned as the period of intensive reconstruction. The budget size during this period was approximately 19 trillion yen, which grew to 25 trillion yen after the FY2013 budget. This was done through multiple supplementary budgets, the establishment of a special account for reconstruction, and the use of reconstruction grants. In addition, the government issued bonds and introduced new taxes related to earthquake recovery. During this period, the disposal of earthquake debris, restoration of destroyed social infrastructure, and livelihood support for disaster victims were intensively implemented. The construction of temporary housing and public disaster housing was also carried out intensively. As a result, restoration from the earthquake was largely accomplished[1].

If restoration has been largely accomplished, the challenge will now be to reconstruction from the disaster. This is a process that will lead to the revitalization and development of the region. Regional development here does not simply mean returning to the pre-disaster state. True regional development means improving the economic strength and livability of the region compared to what it was before the earthquake. It also means that the region is oriented toward a new image that was not seen before the earthquake. The government has set the period from FY2016 to FY2020 as the period of Reconstruction and Creation, which is the final part of the 10-year reconstruction period. And it has announced the "Basic Policy for Recovery from the Great East Japan Earthquake," during the

[1] It should be noted that even in 2024, there are still areas hit by the nuclear accident where it is difficult to return to one's home.

Reconstruction and Creation Period. There, the goal is to realize a reconstruction that will serve as a model for regional creation. To achieve this goal, a new vision for town planning and development-oriented reconstruction measures that are different from those of the past are required. Many challenges exist in implementing them.

The first issue to be addressed is that of policy implementation, such as the goals and instruments of reconstruction policy. In particular, the implementation of development-oriented policies raises the issue of whether the policy goals and instruments can be fully agreed upon by the residents of the affected areas. This is a problem that inevitably arises when implementing any new policy, not limited to reconstruction from disaster. People have different ideas of what reconstruction should look like. Therefore, conflicts between the affected local governments and residents are inevitable.

Second, livelihood support for disaster victims is also an important issue. Although livelihood support for disaster victims is often perceived as a short-term issue, it is also true that there are still people who have not recovered from the disaster. The damage caused by the earthquake tends to be concentrated on certain people, rather than occurring equally among the residents of the affected areas. If we ignore those who have yet to recover from the disaster, there can be no true reconstruction. To overcome these issues, housing, medical and welfare-related programs, and mental care for disaster victims will be important issues during the period of Reconstruction and Creation. In fact, the government's basic policy has also identified mental and physical care and other support for disaster victims as an important issue. The government has formulated "Comprehensive Measures for Supporting Disaster Victims (Health and Lifestyle Support)," which consists of 50 programs.

As described above, the earthquake is a complex event that causes multiple problems, so it is not enough to implement reconstruction policies that pursue economic efficiency. It is also necessary to pursue fairness and reconstruction policies that are rooted in the lives of disaster victims. Therefore, this book addresses the various problems associated with earthquake recovery not only from an economic perspective, but also from the perspectives of social business, mental health, and risk-sharing in order to reduce the regional spread of disaster damage. This examination from multiple perspectives is a major feature of this book[2].

[2] Ito et al. (2011) examine recovery and reconstruction programs from various perspectives as early as the post-disaster stage. Iwata (2011) and Sato and Oguro (2011) also discuss recovery and reconstruction programs from an economic perspective at an early stage after the earthquake. In addition, the Economic Reconstruction Policy Research Committee (2013) is a collection of policy recommendations in which the authors of this book (Shumpei Yaoita and Kazuhiro Yaguchi) also participated.

1.2 Damage from the Earthquake

This book focuses mainly on the recovery from the Great East Japan Earthquake, but also looks at the damage from other earthquakes for comparison. Damage from the Great East Japan Earthquake and other earthquakes is shown below (see Table 1.1).

Each of the three earthquakes has its own characteristics in terms of damage. The Great Hanshin-Awaji Earthquake was the first earthquake to hit a major city. It was the first earthquake in recorded history to register 7 on the Japanese seismic intensity scale. The affected areas were mainly urban areas in Hyogo Prefecture, and the earthquake had the characteristics of an urban earthquake. Damage was characterized by collapsed buildings and large fires. And more than 6000 people died from crushing deaths caused by collapsed buildings. The death toll was 6434, and the estimated amount of damage was approximately 9.6 trillion yen. The collapsed buildings were widely televised on TV and other media at the time. In addition, the Great Hanshin-Awaji Earthquake attracted the attention of many citizens who participated as disaster volunteers. This phenomenon led to 1995, the year of the earthquake, being called the "first year of volunteerism." This led to the enactment of the "NPO Law" in 1998.

Table 1.1 Damage from each earthquake

	Great Hanshin-Awaji Earthquake	Great East Japan Earthquake	Kumamoto Earthquake of 2016
Date of occurrence	January 17, 1995	March 11,2011	April 16, 2016
Magnitude of earthquake	7.2	9.0	7.3
Main affected areas	Hyogo Prefecture	8 prefectures (Iwate, Miyagi, Fukushima, Ibaraki, Tochigi, Gunma, Chiba, and Saitama)	Kumamoto and Oita Prefectures
Characteristics of the affected area	Urban area	Focused on agriculture, forestry, and fisheries areas (especially coastal areas)	All areas of Kumamoto Prefecture (including mountainous areas)
Characteristics of damage	Buildings collapsed, large fires occurred mainly in Nagata Ward, Kobe City.	Large tsunami caused extensive damage in coastal areas	More than half of the deaths were caused by aggravation of injuries or physical strain from living in evacuation shelters, etc.
Deaths	6434 people	19,775 people	277 people
Estimated amount of damage	Approx. 9.6 trillion yen	Approx. 16.9 trillion yen	Approx. 2.4–4.6 trillion yen

Source: Prepared by the author using various data from the Japanese National Police Agency, Fire and Disaster Management Agency, etc.

The Great East Japan Earthquake was the largest earthquake in recorded history, and was referred to as "the second defeat of the war" or "a tragedy once in a thousand years." The earthquake was characterized by the wide geographical scope of the disaster. Damage from the earthquake was concentrated in Iwate, Miyagi, and Fukushima prefectures. The damage was characterized by large tsunamis hitting coastal areas, and drowning deaths from tsunamis were the largest cause of death. Therefore, even within the three affected prefectures, there are differences in damage between coastal and noncoastal areas. In addition, 121,995 houses were totally destroyed and 282,939 houses were partially destroyed. The earthquake killed more than 15,000 people and caused an estimated damage of about 16.9 trillion yen. Thus, the earthquake caused more damage than the other two earthquakes. However, it is said that these damage estimates are based on an overestimation of the damage. It has been pointed out that these overestimates probably influence the government's decisions on reconstruction budgets, leading to excessive reconstruction budgets[3].

There are two characteristics that distinguish the Great East Japan Earthquake from other earthquakes. The first is the impact of the *Fukushima Daiichi Nuclear Power Plant* accident. In areas near the nuclear power plant, people were forced to evacuate and relocate due to evacuation designations and other reasons. This caused excessive psychological stress on the affected people. In addition, the nuclear accident caused harmful rumors. This had a negative impact on Fukushima Prefecture, such as a decrease in sales of agricultural products and a decline in tourism. Second, because the tsunami damage was so severe, the question is how to position tsunami countermeasures in post-disaster urban development and town planning. This is most evident in the issue of the construction of coastal dikes. In fact, in some municipalities, there was friction between the builders and the residents of the affected areas. It is also important to consider how individuals respond when a tsunami occurs. This is an issue related to disaster education and transmission from the past. The impact of these contents on the damage would not be negligible.

At the time of the Great East Japan Earthquake, as in the case of the Great Hanshin-Awaji Earthquake, there were many disaster volunteer participants. Many participants came from the Tokyo metropolitan area and other distant places. As a result, the word *kizuna* (bond), meaning being connected to the disaster area and disaster victims, became widespread.

In the 2016 Kumamoto earthquake, two major earthquakes occurred: the first on the night of April 14, and the second in the early morning of April 16. The Japan Meteorological Agency (JMA) has considered the earthquake on April 14 to be a foreshock and the one on April 16 to be the main earthquake. Seismic activity was active, characterized by more aftershocks than in previous Japanese earthquakes, and tremors were felt in the Kanto and Hokuriku regions during the main quake. The damage was characteristic of a direct earthquake, with collapsed buildings and landslides. Damage was concentrated in old wooden houses built before the revision of the *Building Standards Law* in 1981. In mountainous areas, roads and other social

[3] Harada (2012) and Saito (2015a) point out.

infrastructure were destroyed and evacuation centers were cut off. The number of deaths was 247. More than half of these deaths were attributed to aggravation of injuries from the disaster or physical strain from living in evacuation shelters.

1.3 Overview of Reconstruction Status and Reconstruction Policies

This section describes the status of recovery from the Great East Japan Earthquake. Then, we will introduce the Recovery Plan formulated by Miyagi Prefecture. Furthermore, taking the Kumamoto earthquake as an example, we will introduce the reconstruction plan formulated by Kumamoto Prefecture.

1.3.1 Overview of Reconstruction Status

In June 2015, the Japanese government released "Restoration and Reconstruction Projects for Fiscal 2016 and beyond." The government positioned the period from FY2016 to FY2020 as a "period of reconstruction and creation" and strongly emphasized the perspective of regional creation. The budget for implementing the reconstruction policy is to secure 32 trillion yen in total resources since FY2011. In March 2016, "Basic policy for recovery from the Great East Japan Earthquake during the Reconstruction and Creation Period" was formulated. The issues addressed in this policy are: (1) support for victims' health and livelihood, (2) reconstruction of homes and towns, (3) revitalization of industries and livelihoods, (4) recovery and reconstruction from the nuclear disaster, and (5) "creation of a new Tohoku." In the area of support for disaster victims, the problem of loneliness caused by the loss of their former homes and jobs has led to suicides and alcoholism. Therefore, efforts to address mental health issues, called "mental recovery," were also taken up.

In the second five years of the recovery period, reconstruction has made more progress than in the first half. The Reconstruction Agency (2021) reported that the number of evacuees, which was about 470,000 immediately after the earthquake, had decreased to 171,000 as of March 2016 and to 49,000 as of December 2019. Similarly, it reported that the number of public disaster housing units constructed increased from 300 units at the end of March 2013, two years after the earthquake, to 17,000 units as of March 2016, and to 30,000 units as of December 2020. The initial plan for public disaster housing has been achieved.

Reconstruction progressed on the industrial front as well. Farmland in coastal areas was considerably damaged by the tsunami caused by the earthquake. As of April 2013, only 38% of the area available for resumption of farming operations had increased to 74% as of March 2016 and 94% as of December 2020. In the fish processing industry, 55% of facilities had reopened as of March 2012, but 87% had reopened as of March 2016 and 97% as of December 2020. Furthermore, the recovery of tourism has also progressed. Tourism was severely damaged by harmful rumors about the nuclear power plant accident. The number of foreign overnight stays in the six Tohoku prefectures fell to 36 from the figure of 100 in 2010. Since then, due in part to Japan's inbound effect, the number of foreign tourists reached 128 in 2016 and 255 in 2018, and the sight of foreign tourists is now an everyday sight in the affected areas.

1.3.2 Miyagi Prefecture Earthquake Disaster Recovery Plan

After the Great East Japan Earthquake in March 2011, Miyagi Prefecture established the "Miyagi Prefecture Earthquake Reconstruction Council" and announced the "Miyagi Prefecture Earthquake Disaster Recovery Plan" in October 2011. The basic principles of the reconstruction plan are: (1) to create a disaster-resistant community where people can live with peace of mind, (2) to make each and every citizen of the prefecture the main actor in the reconstruction and to mobilize their collective strength, (3) to go beyond "restoration" to radical reconstruction, (4) to create an advanced community that can solve problems of modern society, and (5) to build a model of reconstruction from the devastating damage. The plan period is 10 years, from FY2011 to FY2020, with FY2011 to FY2013 as the restoration period, FY2014 to FY2015 as the reconstruction period, and FY2018 to FY2020 as the development period.

This plan has been formulated on a time frame that includes the restoration, reconstruction, and development phases. Seven urgent priority items are listed for immediate restoration, including livelihood support for disaster victims and early restoration of lifelines. These seven urgent priority items are restoration projects related to livelihood restoration, in the sense of restoring people's lives to pre-disaster levels. The recovery plan is not limited to restoration to the pre-disaster level, but also includes policies for fundamental restructuring, and programs for regeneration and development. The ten main points of the plan are as follows:

(i) Establishment of the Miyagi Model for Disaster-Resilient City Development
(ii) Reconstruction of Miyagi as a fisheries prefecture
(iii) Establishment of an advanced agriculture and forestry industry
(iv) "Realization of a wealthy Miyagi Prefecture" through early recovery of the manufacturing industry
(v) Revitalization of tourism with diverse attractions
(vi) Reconstruction of health, medical care, and welfare services that encompass the region
(vii) Formation of eco-towns utilizing renewable energy sources
(viii) Promoting the development of disaster-resistant prefectural and national land
(ix) Development of human resources for the future
(x) Establishment of financial resources, systems, and partnerships to support reconstruction

One of the most notable of these reconstruction plans is the "Special Zone for Fisheries Reconstruction" concept discussed in (ii). The concept contemplates the full introduction of private capital into the fisheries industry. In addition, (i) outlines various methods for separating work and residence in coastal areas and relocating to higher ground, while (vii) presents ideas that will lead to the compact city concept.

1.3.3 Plan for Recovery and Reconstruction from the 2016 Kumamoto Earthquake

In response to the 2016 Kumamoto Earthquake, "Plan for Recovery and Restoration from the 2016 Kumamoto Earthquake" was released in August 2016. The basic principle set forth in this plan is to "mobilize the collective efforts of the prefecture's residents to maximize the prefecture's total well-being for future generations."[4] The four initiatives listed here are: (1) reconstruction of lifestyles and livelihoods, (2) restoration of social infrastructure, (3) revitalization of local industries, and (4) restoration of the exchange function. Furthermore, four basic directions for the creation of a new Kumamoto have been set forth. They are as follows:

(i) Creation of secure and hopeful lifestyles ~Achieving peace of mind hope
(ii) Creation of assets for the future ~Laying the foundation for the future
(iii) Creation of strong local industry for the next generation: Revitalizing local vitality and employment
(iv) Creation of a New Kumamoto Connected to the World: Taking on the World and Opening Up the World

In (i), measures related to livelihood support, medical care, and welfare are listed. In addition, programs such as earthquake-proofing of housing and establishment of community-based comprehensive care are also mentioned. In (ii), policies related to urban development and town planning are listed. In (iii), programs related to industrial policy are given. It indicates the need to revitalize the agriculture, forestry, and fisheries industries, which are the main industries of the prefecture. Furthermore, programs for the tourism industry that takes advantage of local resources are also indicated. In (iv), programs to improve the functions of airports and ports in order to make the prefecture a gateway to Asia are listed.

1.4 Issues in Restoration and Reconstruction Policies

In the previous section, we outlined the reconstruction plans of the government and of Miyagi and Kumamoto prefectures. In this section, we discuss three issues that are important in the process of implementing recovery plans, and examine policy issues in analyzing the reconstruction from the disaster[5].

[4] See Kumamoto Prefectural Government (2016).

[5] This section is based on Yaguchi (2013).

1.4.1 Time Frame for Restoration and Reconstruction

Recovery plans for disaster stricken areas often set restoration as a short-term issue and reconstruction as a medium- to long-term issue. This concept was expressed in discussions at the government's Reconstruction Design Council immediately after the earthquake. It pointed out the importance of presenting restoration and reconstruction policies with a time frame in mind. This approach was also followed in the government's basic policy, which sets the five-year period following the earthquake as the period of restoration and the subsequent five-year period as the period of reconstruction and creation. It is correct as a methodology to implement restoration and reconstruction policies on a timeline. The recovery plans of Miyagi and Kumamoto prefectures also consist of short-term restoration programs and medium- to long-term reconstruction programs.

However, issues such as livelihood support and rebuilding the lives of disaster victims are not only a matter of restoration but also of reconstruction. In a situation where livelihood reconstruction is not in place, reconstruction policies that talk about a vision for the future will not be accepted honestly by residents and businesses in the affected areas. Some argue that rebuilding livelihoods is of utmost importance in the affected areas, and that reconstruction cannot be seen without rebuilding livelihoods[6]. While it is necessary to establish a time frame for the short, medium, and long term, there is no clear distinction between actual restoration policies and reconstruction policies.

Each year, Miyagi Prefecture conducts a survey of prefectural residents' attitudes. In the 2019 survey, a high percentage of responses cited securing the living environment and livelihood support as priority reconstruction programs. While these issues are restorative aspects, they are also issues that are linked to reconstruction. As long as these issues are left behind, there will be no understanding of the medium- to long-term reconstruction policies for the affected disaster areas.

1.4.2 Relationship between Reconstruction Policies and Local Problems

In general, the recovery plans of affected municipalities commonly include an exhaustive list of restoration and reconstruction policies. The damage caused by the earthquake and tsunami is enormous in scope and quantity. The damage caused by the earthquake was enormous in both scope and quantity. There is no doubt that this will require a multifaceted policy. However, the exhaustive nature of restoration and reconstruction policies can lead to a loss of focus on what needs to be done.

---

[6] Sekiya (2011) pointed out immediately after the earthquake.

Taking Miyagi Prefecture as an example, this section corresponds to points (ii) through (v) of the Miyagi Prefecture Earthquake Disaster Recovery Plan. The actual programs mentioned here are the state of agriculture and fisheries, economic development and job creation centered on the manufacturing industry, and promotion of tourism. These programs are related to reconstruction in the sense that they anticipate the regeneration and development of the region beyond the damage caused by the earthquake. And they are at the core of the reconstruction programs. However, these issues were already recognized as prefectural issues before the earthquake. Some of the programs were already in place before the earthquake, and are not particularly new. Before the earthquake, Miyagi Prefecture had been concerned about its dependence on the service industry. In order to shift away from such a character, the prefecture has emphasized the growth of agriculture, fisheries, and manufacturing industries. Even after the earthquake, this direction has not changed. In light of this, the Miyagi's recovery plan provided an excellent opportunity to strengthen the existing policy agenda. Based on this interpretation, this plan can be viewed as an addition of disaster, eco-town, and new energy policies to the existing policy issues.

Whether or not existing policy issues and town planning efforts can become recovery policy is another matter. In this sense, the recovery plan of not only Miyagi Prefecture but also many other disaster stricken municipalities have the same characteristics. With the exception of programs that need to be implemented urgently, the plan is likely to be nothing more than a continuation of existing policy issues and the addition of reconstruction programs related to the earthquake disaster. Although it appears to be a multifaceted recovery plan, in reality it is merely a continuation of the various programs that have been implemented in the past. This would leave us in a situation where the reconstruction policy and the regional policy that have been implemented from the past are almost identical.

1.4.3 Role-Sharing of Market and Government

In implementing restoration and reconstruction policies, the role of the government is sometimes overly expected. In light of the earthquake disaster, it is true that only the government can play a role in urgent matters. However, it is not necessarily the case that only the government can implement restoration and reconstruction policies. This is also reflected in the government's basic policies for reconstruction. This policy emphasizes the importance of reconstruction through the power of the private sector. Specifically, this policy indicates the importance of funds and public–private partnerships (PPPs) that leverage private-sector funds and expertise. In fact, public–private partnerships have been adopted in public infrastructure such as disaster public housing and urban parks. Furthermore, the task is to promote the activities of NPOs, volunteers, and the fire brigades and community welfare volunteers who have supported the community. Thus, there is no necessity for the government to make a full-scale appearance in all reconstruction efforts.

In this regard, it is important to distinguish between an economic policy and a social policy. An economic policy should be aimed at strengthening the economic power of the region. Specific programs include fostering industry, inducing employment, and deregulation. On the other hand, a social policy is concerned with rebuilding the lives of disaster victims and includes income compensation and housing provision. These two policies are not necessarily in conflict with each other. Sato and Oguro (2011) argue as follows. "Economic policy = market-oriented and competition-oriented, and social policy = support for the vulnerable in the event of a disaster are not two separate but rather complementary, and economic policy and social policy are the two wheels of recovery."[7] We believe this idea is necessary to implement policies for restoration and reconstruction from the disaster.

1.5 Composition of This Book

The book consists of this chapter and five others, many of which are analyzed by economics. Chapter 2 discusses the characteristics and advantages of social business. It shows that private companies can play a role in creating social value through commerce. This chapter introduces examples of social business in the areas affected by the Great East Japan Earthquake. Based on interviews with people in the affected areas, this chapter makes policy recommendations for the promotion of social business. Here, the author argues for the effectiveness of commerce through social business to address the problem of shrinking economic circulation due to supply constraints in the affected areas. Chapter 3 discusses urban development and town planning after the Great East Japan Earthquake. The main focus here is on reconstruction town planning along the lines of compact cities and the coastal dikes issue. This chapter examines the promotion of compact cities from a theoretical and policy perspective. Urban economic externalities must occur for compact cities to be efficient in resource allocation. The study also shows that promoting compact cities must be done in conjunction with public transportation policies.

Chapter 4 addresses mental health issues. In general, the problems of the earthquake are not only economic problems. People's mental problems are also earthquake damage. As one of these, this chapter addresses the problem of alcohol dependence among disaster victims. After the Great East Japan Earthquake, the number of consultations concerning alcohol dependence has increased. Alcohol dependence caused by the loss of one's home, separation from family, and loss of employment due to the disaster is difficult to counteract with forced sobriety. In addition, it creates a sense of fatigue that is similar to burnout in those who are helping people overcome alcohol dependence. For this reason, this chapter argues that support from mental health professionals will be important in the fight against alcohol dependence.

[7] Sato and Oguro (2011) 64p.

The study in Chaps. 5 and 6 are based on analysis using analysis of economics. Chapter 5 focuses on seismic retrofitting of homes. Seismic retrofitting of housing is essential in saving lives. If houses are not earthquake-proof, external diseconomies will occur, which will require policy assistance. We measure the willingness to pay for seismic retrofitting of a home. By doing so, we measure whether the seismic retrofitting of homes is profitable for the firms that rent the homes. Based on those analyses, we propose a method for setting the amount of subsidy. The last chapter, Chap. 6, discusses the regional spread of disaster damage and risk-sharing methods to reduce the risk. The Great East Japan Earthquake considerably destroyed factories and other production facilities in the affected areas. This led to disruptions in the supply chain, and the damage extended to other regions as well.

1.6 Novelty Aspect of This Book

This book contains analyses based on various academic fields and is not limited to economics. Specifically, reconstruction and regeneration after the Great East Japan Earthquake in the Tohoku Area are examined from the viewpoint of the economy, industries, social business, city planning, housing, and mental health.

This book is different from other studies on reconstruction after the Great East Japan Earthquake. For example, Saito (2015a, b) includes approaches from economics, not from mental health.

In terms of economics, Saito (2015b) analyzes the differences between reality and the policymaker's understanding of the amount of damage and the magnitude of the nuclear power plant crisis. Genda (2015) deals with the contents and effects of employment majors chosen after the Great East Japan Earthquake. Our book mainly deals with industrial policy, city planning, housing policy, and regional cooperation using economics. In Chap. 2, we focus on social business, an analysis of business study, which is probably the first attempt in a book on economics about the affected area. Chapter 3 explores desirable town planning and transportation policy in the affected area, while Chap. 4 newly includes psychological research on the mental health of victims of the Great East Japan Earthquake. Chapter 5 examines whether tax cut or subsidy is superior as a source of financial support to improve earthquake-proof conversion of rental housing. Chapter 6 presents a spatial computable general equilibrium model, wherein decrease in regional income through investment in disaster prevention, recovery, and reconstruction is endogenous, which is another novel aspect of the book.

This book focuses on reconstruction and regeneration after the moment of earthquake recovery. That is, removal of earthquake rubble, maintenance of destroyed infrastructure, construction of emergency provisional housing for disaster prevention, and reopening of the schools after the earthquake are almost finished. The Tohoku region faces medium- to long-term issues, such as industrial construction, urban development after the earthquake, earthquake-proof conversion of housing, and freeing oneself from mental illness caused by the earthquake. The focus then shifts to a period later than that of Tohoku University (2012), which deals with the removal and reconstruction period.

Another characteristic of this book is that the six authors of the six chapters are currently conducting research in the devastated region; they lived in the Tohoku region at the time of the Great East Japan Earthquake and have connections with people in the region. In this sense, this book contains research findings from Tohoku based on actual situations of the damaged area after the Great East Japan Earthquake.

In the book, a novel method to estimate the required financial support for improvements is proposed and compares the efficacy of tax incentives versus subsidies for promoting earthquake-proof conversions of rental housing. Combining the contingent valuation method and the discounted cash flow method, a model to examine consumers' evaluation of earthquake-proof conversions of rental houses and determine a rental firm's profits following such conversions is proposed.

Researchers who have majored in economics and psychology have made policy proposals and concrete ideas to reconstruct the Tohoku region after the Great East Japan Earthquake. Thus, the book contains not only theoretical but also practical analyses suggesting ways to deal with future earthquakes in general.

The findings and methods of our book are as follows.

In Chap. 2, our findings show that collective impact social businesses undertaken through both public and private sector are indispensable for the area affected by the Great East Japan Earthquake, because they can realize community development, job creation and resolve regional issues in the affected area. The three possible problems of social business are subsidy trap, the valley of death, and market size. The aforementioned findings are mainly drawn from analyses of interviews with leaders of social business in the area affected by the Great East Japan Earthquake.

In Chap. 3, we find that compact cites form effective models for urban development and town planning in the reconstruction of the affected areas, considering the declining population and severe fiscal constraints. A microeconomic analysis in this chapter reveals that the compact city policies contribute to efficient resource allocation if external economic effects of high-level use of central districts are realized. We suggest public transportation policies to promote Bus Rapid Transit systems are important for compact cities in the affected areas, where the increasing older population is unable to travel by car. Moreover, plans incorporating disaster prevention and mitigation measures in the affected areas are presented. We show examples of a system that passes on the lessons learned from the earthquake to future generations.

In Chap. 4, based on research on status quo of the affected areas and interviews with supporters and members of self-help groups, methods to alleviate alcohol-related problems are proposed, considering the rapid increase in the aging population, shortage of experienced supporters, geographical problems, and depopulation in the affected areas. We find the need to establish and use a remote connection environment to support the alcohol addicted people and the supporters of them through creation of new networks in the affected areas.

In Chap. 5, we propose a method to estimate the required financial support for improvements, combining the contingent valuation method (CVM) and the discounted cash flow method (DCF). The former is used to estimate a consumer's evaluation of earthquake-proof conversion of housing. When this method was applied to analyze rental apartments in Tokyo and Miyagi Prefectures, it revealed a shortfall in profitability in implementing earthquake-proof conversion for rental firms, emphasizing the need for financial support to bolster earthquake resilience in rental housing in Japan. Drawing from this analysis, a method to determine the requisite financial support for earthquake-proof conversions is proposed, evaluating the merits of municipal fixed property tax reduction versus subsidy provision. These findings offer valuable insights for policymakers, presenting strategies to incentivize earthquake-proof conversions and enhance disaster preparedness in the housing sector.

Finally, in Chap. 6, we develop a spatial computable general equilibrium (SCGE) model to measure the damage caused by the Great East Japan Earthquake and the effects of reconstruction investment and public insurance on social welfare, real GDP, and production output. The results reveal that natural disasters and reconstruction investment have asymmetric spillover effects on income.

During reconstruction and regeneration, after recovery from the earthquake, we need to construct a design for the future so that when disaster strikes, the damage to any city or region can be handled with preparedness on all fronts, especially focusing on the economic base that the devastated area should own.

The findings showed that, even 13 years after the Great East Japan Earthquake, disparity was seen among inhabitants in the region, with many people in the devastated areas not having stable employment, and some becoming mentally distressed and alcohol-dependent. Feelings of alienation and helplessness have caused problems on their road to recovery on other fronts.

Our aim is to evaluate and examine what has been done in the period of recovery and reconstruction after the Great East Japan Earthquake and propose new resolutions for development, ensuring safety, and preventing any further mental agony for the affected people.

References

Genda, Y. (2015) *Kiki to Koyo—Saigai no Rodo Keizaigaku—[Crisis and Employment—Labor Economics of Disaster],* Tokyo: Iwanami Shoten.

Harada, Y. (2012) *Shinsai Fukkou Giman no Kouzu,* Tokyo: Shintyousya.

Ito, S. et al. (2011) *Higashinihondaishinsai Fukkou he no Teigen,* Tokyo: Tokyo Daigaku Shuppankai.

Iwata, K. (2011) *Keizaifukkou:Daishinsai kara Tachiagaru,* Tokyo: Tikuma Syobo.

Kumamoto Prefectural Government (2016) *Heisei 28nen Kumamoto Jishin karano Fukkkyu Fukkou Plan.*

Miyagi Prefectural Government (2011) *Miyagi Prefecture Earthquake Disaster Recovery Plan: The Bond between Miyagi, Tohoku and Japan from Recovery to Prosperity —<summary>.*

Reconstruction Agency (2021) *Fukkou no Genzyou to Kadai.*

Reconstruction Design Council in response to the Great East Japan Earthquake (2011) *Towards Reconstruction "Hope beyond the Disaster,"* 25 June 2011 Report to the Prime Minister of Reconstruction, Design Council in response to the Great East Japan Earthquake.

Saito, M. (2015a) *Shinsai Fukko no Seijikeizaigaku—Tsynamihisai to Genpatukiki no Bunri to Kosaku [Political Economics of Recovery from the Earthquake—Separation and Mixture of Nuclear Power Plant Crisis and Tsunami Damages—],* Tokyo: Nippon Hyoron Sha.

Saito, M. (2015b) *Shinsai to Keizai [The Economy and the Earthquake],* Tokyo: Toyo Keizai Inc.

Sato, M. and K. Oguro (2011) *Shinsaifukkou: Jishinsaigai ni Tsuyoi Syakai Keizai no Kouchiku,* Tokyo: Nippon Hyouronsya.

Sekiya, N. (2011) "Seikatsusaiken ga Sangyousaisei he no Michisuji-Chiiki no Sangyou Fukkou to Koyoukakuho wo Dousuruka," *Kaikakusha*, June 2011, 34–37.

The Economic Reconstruction Policy Research Committee (2013) *Higashinihondaishinsai karano Fukkou Saisei no tameno Seisakuteigen,* Tokyo: Seisaku Kenkyu Forum.

Tohoku University ed. (2012) *Higashinihon Daishinsai Fukko Kenkyu I [Research on Recovery after the Great East Japan Earthquake I]*, Sendai: Nanboku sha.

Yaguchi, K. (2013) "The Point at Issue in Policy Process of Recovery Plan and Reconstruction Policy from Higashi-Nihon Great Earthquake," *Kokyo Sentaku (Public Choice Studies),* 59, 126–142.

Chapter 2
Social Business in the Great East Japan Earthquake and Regional Revitalization

Shumpei Yaoita

Abstract This chapter reviewed the population situation in affected areas based on census results and the changing political leadership 13 years after the Great East Japan Earthquake. In this context, we examined the challenges in the promotion of business, especially social business, in affected areas, such as the "subsidy trap," the "valley of death," and the "market size problem." Given that huge budgets have been allocated for reconstruction in the areas affected by the Great East Japan Earthquake, it is important to link "work" and "community development," while changing the approach to subsidies and social business development projects for their most effective use. Thirteen years after the Great East Japan Earthquake, reconstruction has entered a new stage. This implies that subsidies and social businesses must also change. As the population continues to decline, social business will play a major role in the new "creative reconstruction."

Keywords Social business · Collective impact · Subsidy trap · The valley of death · Market size problem

S. Yaoita (✉)
College of Regional Development, Shukutoku University, Saitama, Japan
e-mail: shumpei-yaoita@u.shukutoku.ac.jp

K. N. Hirono, K. Yaguchi (eds.), *Reconstruction Period and the Stages of Regeneration After a Great Earthquake*, New Frontiers in Regional Science: Asian Perspectives 83, https://doi.org/10.1007/978-981-96-8822-7_2

2.1 Introduction[1]

In this chapter, we will look at the definition and issues surrounding social business. The situation in the affected areas is changing. As reconstruction shifts from a focus on the infrastructure to the local economy and local community, it is thought that social businesses that solve local issues and encourage entrepreneurship in the affected areas will be important. Therefore, it is thought that identifying and examining the issues of entrepreneurship and social businesses will be of great significance for future reconstruction and regional revitalization.

Thirteen years have passed since the Great East Japan Earthquake occurred. Subsequent earthquakes with a recorded intensity of 7 on the Japanese seismic intensity scale were the Kumamoto Earthquake in 2016, and the Hokkaido Bold East Earthquake in 2018. Most recently, the Noto Earthquake occurred in January 2024. In addition, there is growing concern about Nankai Trough earthquakes and earthquakes occurring directly under the Tokyo metropolitan area.

The Great East Japan Earthquake was characterized by the combined effects of the tsunami and the Fukushima nuclear disaster. Sweeping along the Pacific coast of eastern Japan from Iwate to Chiba Prefectures, the tsunami caused extensive damage, including damage to the Fukushima nuclear power plant. Together with the forced evacuation of residents from neighboring areas, the scars from the earthquake run deep, and continue to have an impact today, 13 years later. While the Japanese government has invested a large amount of money in affected areas, particularly the Iwate, Miyagi, and Fukushima prefectures, and has been working on reconstruction efforts, the recovery from the Great East Japan Earthquake remains a work in progress.

In terms of hardware (social infrastructure), land was raised, breakwaters constructed, and streets rehabilitated. As a result, the current landscape in some areas has changed dramatically compared to before the earthquake. For instance, the construction of breakwaters for safety reasons inevitably change the landscape of people's "hometowns," which no longer seem the same.

In the debate over whether to "return to the original town" or "create a new town," the older generation preferred the "return" option, while the younger generation was more in favor of the "new" option. These differing opinions impose a heavy burden of "time cost" on consensus building and town planning for reconstruction, and even lead to conflict at times.

In addition, as time passes after a disaster, residents may develop the feeling that reconstruction is not progressing as they had initially hoped. Consequently,

---

[1] In writing this report, we interviewed Naohiro Nakagawa (Representative Director, Public interest incorporated foundation of JAPAN CHALLENGER PROJECT), Daisuke Matsui (President, Oriai), and Sawa Yatagawa; I would like to thank them for their time and effort. I would also like to thank KAKENHI Scientific Research C, "Research on Quantitative Verification of Regional Development Policies."

dissatisfaction with leaders accumulates, resulting in leadership changes through elections. This can cause further divisions among residents with differing opinions.

Another important aspect of reconstruction is ensuring a stable population; even if progress is made in the city's reconstruction, if the population declines, the city will lose its liveliness. Therefore, it is necessary to increase the local population and revitalize the economy through consumption activities. In order to increase the resident population, both "job creation" and "community development" are crucial. The concept of "social business" is key in linking "work" and "community development."

2.2 Changes in the Disaster Area

With 13 years having passed since the Great East Japan Earthquake, it is important to review the population and aging status in the affected areas of Iwate, Miyagi, and Fukushima prefectures. Based on national census statistics, Figs. 2.1, 2.2 and 2.3 summarize the changes in these areas regarding the population[2] and aging rate[3] from 2010 to 2020.

In Iwate Prefecture, only Takizawa City and Yakin Town experienced population growth over the past decade, whereas other municipalities experienced population decline. Especially in coastal areas, the population is declining and the aging rate is high. For example, in Rikuzentakata City, the population in 2020 was approximately 20 points lower than in 2010, with an aging rate of 40.28% (see Fig. 2.1.).

The situation in Miyagi Prefecture is varied. Sendai City, Natori City, Tomiya City, Taiwa Town, and Ohira Village are experiencing population growth with an aging rate in the 20% range. Meanwhile, the population in the earthquake affected area of Onagawa Town was approximately 35 points lower in 2020 than in 2010, and the aging rate was 36.3%. In Shichigasuku, Marumori, Yamamoto, and Minamisanriku, the population in 2020 was also some 20–30 points lower than in 2010, and the aging rate was in the 40% range. The population in Ishinomaki City and Kesennuma City is also expected to be approximately 15 points lower in 2020 compared to 2010 (see Fig. 2.2.).

The situation in Fukushima Prefecture must be divided into nuclear disaster-affected areas[4] and other areas. If we focus on the areas affected by the nuclear disaster, Okuma, Namie, Tomioka, Naraha, Katsurao, and Iitate villages clearly have significantly smaller populations in 2020 than they did in 2010. The 2020 aging rate in Iitate Village was over 50%, while in Katsurao Village it was 47.1%, and in Naraha Machi, it was 37.1%. These conditions have a significant impact on the sustainability of the region (see Fig. 2.3.).

[2] Seen as the difference between the 2010 census results and the 2020 census results, with an increase above 100% indicating an increase and a decrease below 100% indicating a decrease.

[3] The aging rate is based on data from the 2020 census results.

[4] Futaba Town was excluded because census results were not shown.

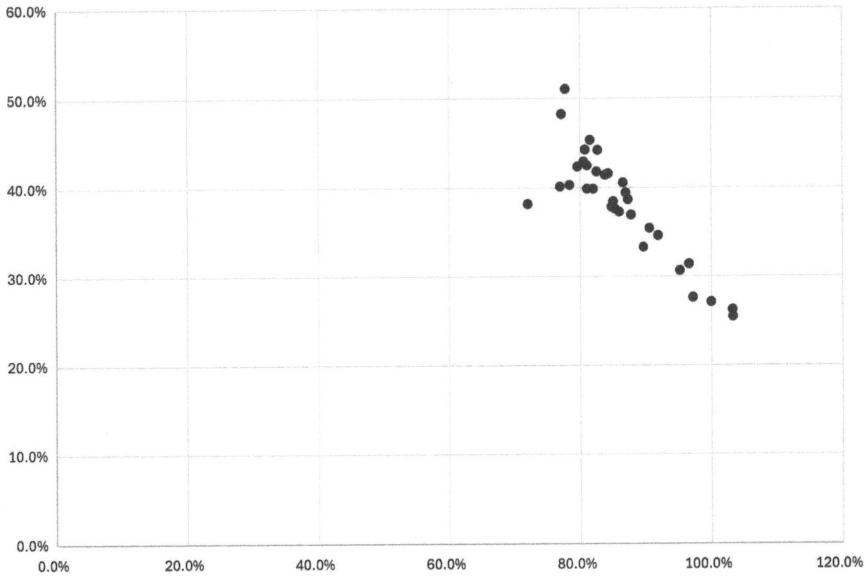

Fig. 2.1 Population change and aging rate in Iwate Prefecture. Source: Prepared by the author based on 2010 and 2020 Census results (Statistics Bureau, Ministry of Internal Affairs and Communications)

While it is clear that areas affected by the Great East Japan Earthquake are experiencing population decline and aging, the reason for this is slightly complex. In fact, it is likely that rather than being caused by the Great East Japan Earthquake, the population phenomena would have occurred as a long-term trend even without the earthquake. In this case, reconstruction in areas affected by the Great East Japan Earthquake has made progress on the hardware side, but has not been able to halt the long-term trends of population decline and aging.

With large-scale subsidies invested by the government and other sources, progress has been made on the hardware side of the reconstruction project over the past decade. However, as residents' sentiments change and their needs become more detailed, together with a declining and aging population, in this context, the promotion of social business is considered to be important.

2.3 Reconstruction and Regional Revitalization

Given that population decline and aging are not trends in only the areas affected by the Great East Japan Earthquake, but in the country as a whole, Japan began a policy of regional development in 2014. The goal of regional development is to create attractive areas in each region through ingenuity and proactive efforts, in order to alleviate the concentration of the population in the Tokyo area, and revitalize local

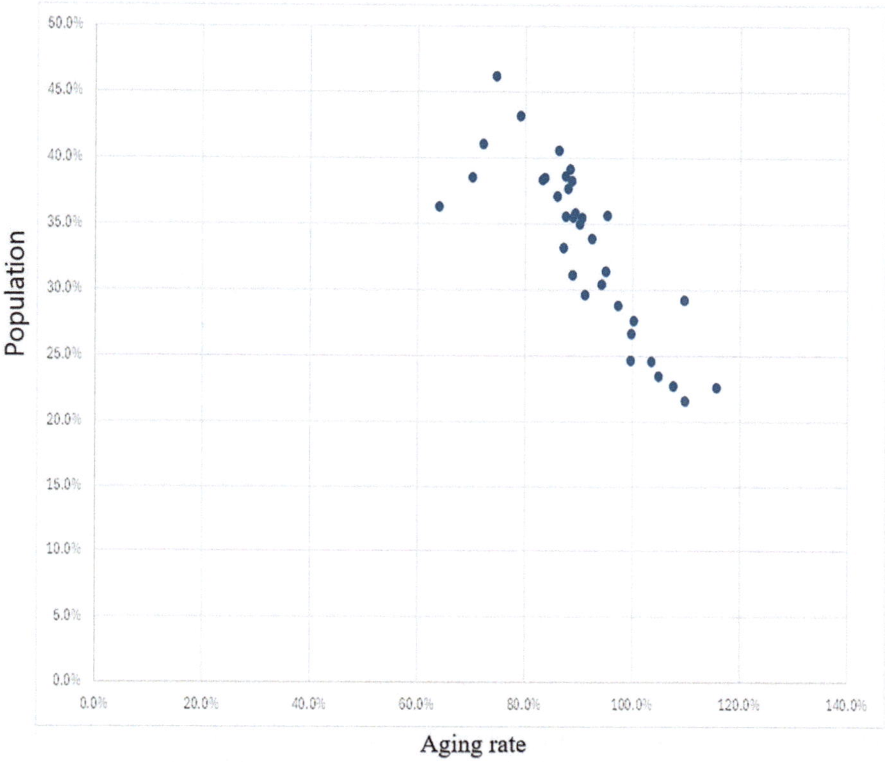

Fig. 2.2 Population change and aging rate in Miyagi Prefecture. Source: Prepared by the author based on 2010 and 2020 Census results (Statistics Bureau, Ministry of Internal Affairs and Communications)

economies. Yaoita (2017) defined a local development policy as a comprehensive policy comprising population and urban issues, economic policy, and regional policy.

While the Great East Japan Earthquake reconstruction efforts target earthquake affected areas, regional development targets the entire nation. In other words, the areas affected by the Great East Japan Earthquake are naturally also targets of regional development, and have thus seen the promotion of both reconstruction and regional development efforts.

Local economy and population influence each other. When the local economy is revitalized, the number of "jobs" will increase and the population will grow, and when the population grows, consumption activities within the region will increase, in turn revitalizing the local economy. Creating this virtuous cycle is necessary for both reconstruction and regional development.

One measure adopted to revitalize the local economy has been attracting companies and factories to the area. Attracting large companies and factories to a region can increase employment, increase consumption by employees and their families, and increase demand in the region. Furthermore, this will also lead to an increase in

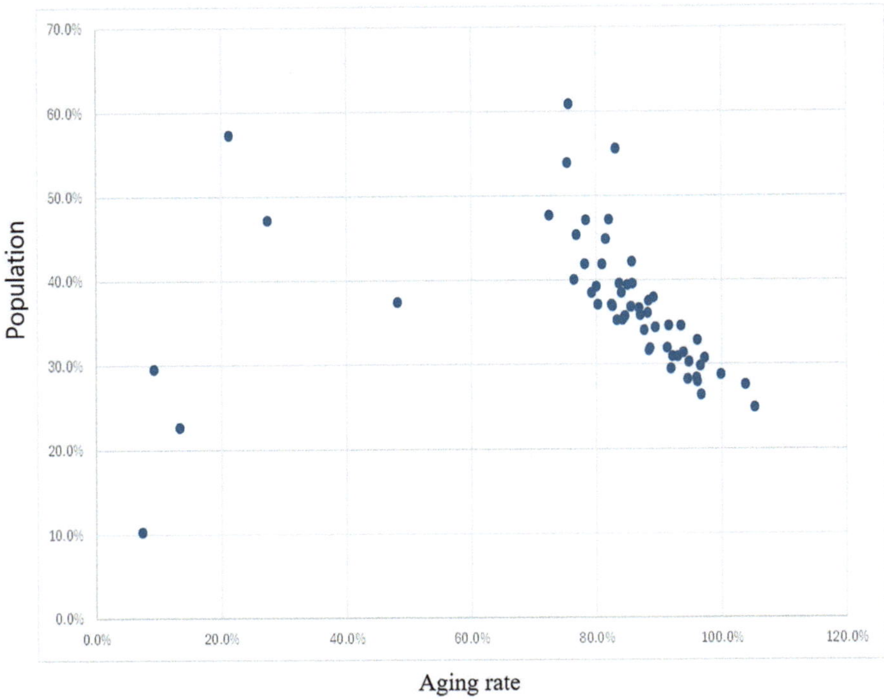

Fig. 2.3 Population change and aging rate in Fukushima Prefecture. Source: Prepared by the author based on 2010 and 2020 Census results (Statistics Bureau, Ministry of Internal Affairs and Communications)

municipal tax revenues, including property, corporate enterprise, and corporate inhabitant taxes. Since the end of World War II, "corporate castle towns" have been established in various regions of Japan, contributing to the development of local communities and economies. Nevertheless, there are certain risks associated with this, such as the withdrawal of these companies, which are the driving force behind the local economy. For example, the overseas relocation of such companies in the 1990s led to the hollowing out of local industries. Efforts by local governments to attract companies and factories are essential for regional development. However, this discussion cannot be conducted without considering enhancing the region's own earning power.

If we consider population movement (migration) as an example, its major factors include higher education, employment, job change, marriage, childbirth, child-rearing, and educational opportunities for children.[5] A population increase in the region, either through an increase in birth rate or an increase in the inflow of people, requires the key factors of "education" and "work."

[5] See Nakazawa et al. (2016) for a discussion of the relationship between the child-rearing environment (e.g., childcare services) and population mobility.

For example, the absence of a local high school within commuting distance will require young people in the area to move for educational purposes. Therefore, the presence of a high school not only provides educational opportunities, but also has the effect of keeping young people in the community. This is also true of universities.

With regard to child-rearing, nuclear families are increasingly the norm, making it difficult for parents, especially working couples, to raise children within the family alone, and hence requiring the use of local child-rearing services. The case of Nagareyama City, Chiba Prefecture, is a good example of the effect of child-rearing services on increasing population inflow. For this reason, local governments in Japan are competitively enhancing their child-rearing environments and policies.

Increasing a region's earning power and enhancing services that solve local problems are thus key factors affecting its sustainability. This is directly related to "social business."

2.4 What Is Social Business?

The concept of social business, as proposed by Dr. Muhammad Yunus, the 2006 Nobel Peace Prize laureate, is finding "a way to solve some social problem through business methods." According to this concept, business methods are more effective than NPOs in solving social problems.

The reasons for this, according to Yunus (2010), is that NPOs' reliance on donations, grants, and subsidies as the source of funds for their activities, requires the effort and time originally available for problem-solving to be instead used in obtaining funds; this reduces "problem-solving ability." With business methods, all effort and time can be allocated to solving problems without reducing the problem-solving ability.

In fact, my own experience regarding the effort and time required for grant applications, screening, reporting, and so on, has frequently led me to think that if I could do it with my own money, I would prefer it that way. In my opinion, Dr. Yunus' ideas are compelling.

The "social business" considered here is thus defined as "a business that aims to solve social and regional issues," based on Dr. Yunus' philosophy.

Examples of social business in child-rearing, aging, and regional revitalization can be considered as follows. Child-rearing issues include childcare support, childcare services, childcare services for school-aged children, and learning support. Regarding aging issues, nursing care services, home medical services, transportation support for the elderly, shopping services, and creating places for the elderly to stay were cited. Furthermore, businesses such as regional trading companies can be mentioned from the perspective of specializing in revitalizing local economies.

Until now, such businesses have been considered "community businesses" in Japan. According to the Kanto Bureau of Economy, Trade, and Industry, "community businesses are defined as "initiatives in which local residents proactively solve local issues using business methods".[6] As the Kanto Bureau of Economy, Trade and Industry explains, the relationship between "social business" and "community business" is that "community business" is characterized by its focus on local issues while being included within "social business." Based on this, "social business" can be classified into the following two categories.

1. Community Business Type: Businesses that specialize in solving social and regional issues through business methods by individuals, small businesses, NPOs, etc.
2. Collective Impact Type: Projects that are undertaken through PPPs (Public Private Partnerships) and collective impact in which diverse entities co-create.

Riku Cafe, a nonprofit organization active in Rikuzentakata City, has contributed to health promotion in the aging community by providing "low-sodium, low-calorie" healthy lunches. It also promoted interactions within the community through events and classes.[7]These activities can be categorized as "community business type."

The example of the collaboration between Kirin Holdings and Tono City can also be said to be a social business of the collective impact type. Tono City created the "Beer Village Creation Council," whereby not only producers, but also local government, companies, and other related parties in the city are working together to develop craft beer using hops and other ingredients produced in Tono, tourism, and holding events.[8]

Regional trading companies and tourism trading companies can also be considered "collective impact" social businesses. Regional trading companies are business entities that cooperate with local governments, local financial institutions, local producers, and related parties to sell agricultural products, traditional crafts, and other regional specialties to large consumption centers domestically and overseas. Tourism trading companies, which are also part of regional trading companies, work with local governments, financial institutions, and stakeholders to plan sightseeing tours and events, market them overseas and outside the region, and increase the number of tourists and other visitors to the region. These can be described as "connector/hub companies."

These "social businesses" are characterized by three points: First, social businesses are businesses that address social and regional issues. Since reconstruction is also a regional issue, social business is not only a driving force for reconstruction itself, but also creates "jobs" and contributes to the revitalization of the regional economy. In other words, "needs" from the demand side are "business opportunities" from the supply side. This is the starting point of social businesses.

Second, these "social businesses" create "jobs" together with "community value" by solving local issues. In other words, they have the function of connecting and

---

[6] https://www.kanto.meti.go.jp/seisaku/cb/index.html

[7] In recent years, due to the new coronavirus infection, many activities have been suspended and lunch is now available as takeout. http://rikucafe.jp/

[8] https://www.city.tono.iwate.jp/index.cfm/4653172296.html

balancing "work" and "community development." In particular, the "collective impact type" business is the "core" linking "work" and "community development."

Third, "social business" is inseparable from the concepts of "social capital" and "community." Social capital refers to social relationships such as "trust," "reciprocity," and "networks," which, in turn, affect economic output (Putnam, 1993, 2000). Social capital has a significant impact on solving social and community problems. Moreover, it is important to note that if commonality and homogeneity exist in a community in terms of familial relationships, such as blood ties, regional characteristics, associated geographical ties, and cultural backgrounds, they impact the strength of the community. For instance, even among groups with "homogeneity," some have established relationships of trust and reciprocity, while others do not.

In other words, a community with a high quality of social capital is a strong "community," and a community with low-quality social capital is a weak "community." This affects the basis of "collective impact."

"Collective impact" is an approach in which diverse actors organically work together to solve problems through continuous communication, with common goals, common evaluation and measurement methods, and mutually complementary plans. Collective impact can serve as a theoretical background for initiatives such as collaboration and co-creation.

In other words, solving social and regional issues requires a strong "community" where high quality social capital exists. This strong "community" will serve as a foundation to bring out the effects of "collective impact," which will connect "work" and "community development," and enhance the problem-solving ability of "social business" in addressing regional and social issues.

In this chapter, the concept of social business is broadly defined as business that aims to solve local and social issues, and includes companies and entrepreneurs. If we were to distinguish between a general joint-stock company and a social business, we could find the difference in the profit distribution system.

In the case of a general company, a profit distribution system is necessary to distribute profits to shareholders. However, in the case of a social business, a profit distribution system is necessary even if it is a general company. However, by obtaining the approval of shareholders and creating a system that allows the distribution rate to be lowered and as much of the remaining profits as possible to be used for business activities, it will be possible to increase the power to solve issues in the community and society. Also, if it is a social business run by an NPO, it will not be possible to create a profit distribution system in the first place, so it will be possible to use the profits for business activities. This is a significant benefit of expanding social business.

2.5 The Problem of Social Business

As a business entity connecting "work" and "community development" to solve social and regional issues, social business is indispensable for the reconstruction of the areas affected by the Great East Japan Earthquake.

The drivers of these "social businesses" are not limited to local residents; in fact, it is expected that new businesses will be started by regional development cooperatives and immigrants. Regional development cooperation corps[9] is a program promoted by the national government in which local governments recruit local people, pay them wages, and support their projects during their term of office. The budget for the program is allocated by the local government through a local allocation tax subsidy, making the program easy for local governments to use. The aim is for the project to be stabilized during the term of office, after which it will run on its own. However, many issues remain to be solved in this regard.

In addition, although not limited to social business, from the perspective of regional entrepreneurship, three issues should be identified for the future promotion of social business: the "subsidy trap," the "valley of death issue," and "market size."

2.5.1 Subsidy Trap

The town of Okuma in Fukushima Prefecture established an incubation center to support companies and entrepreneurs. The Okuma Incubation Center assigns staff with consulting experience in the private sector as incubation managers, who consistently select companies to be invited to the center to support companies and entrepreneurs, conduct regular interviews, and collaborate with other companies that have moved in. In addition, there are a variety of subsidies and support programs, such as the subsidy program by the Fukushima Prefecture Reconstruction Center, the support program by the 12 Municipal Immigration Support Centers operated by the Fukushima Innovation Coast Initiative Promotion Organization,[10] and support programs unique to each municipality. Programs subsidized by private organizations are also in place.

However, one staff member involved in entrepreneurship support in Okuma Town told us that many towns promote entrepreneurship rather than employment; therefore, most of the support is for start-ups, such as covering start-up costs and employment, with little support for working capital. At the same time, many of the

[9] Okuma Town has a larger budget than other municipalities due to the reconstruction budget and compensation from TEPCO, so it is not eligible for a local tax subsidy and does not have a regional development cooperative program. Therefore, "reconstruction support staff" are assigned to regional development corporations and private companies and are engaged in regional development.

[10] Unique assistance programs for 12 municipalities that have been ordered to evacuate.

programs are designed for returnees and out-of-prefecture migrants, resulting in the impression of little support for migration within Fukushima Prefecture.

Through the interviews for Mr. Nakagawa and Mr. Matsui, also learned that the issue of "monetization" is a major challenge. Even if a company receives considerable start-up support, if it does not "monetize," the business cannot continue. It is, therefore, necessary to create a "monetization" mechanism that can run on its own by the end of the subsidy period. At the same time, the existence of subsidies may make certain businesses dependent and unable to continue on their own after the subsidy period ends.

In fact, this "subsidy trap" has become a major challenge for affected areas, with a tendency for people to get stuck within the system of subsidies and grants. This prevents them from learning to operate on their own, especially when the subsidy ends.

2.5.2 *Valley of Death Problem*

The "valley of death" is a problem in which, as a business expands, it becomes unable to continue its operations because of a lack of working capital. In particular, because the due date for payment on purchases differs from the due date for the collection of sales, even if the company is financially profitable, the due date for payment on purchases comes before the due date for the collection of sales, resulting in insufficient funds on hand, and an inability to pay for purchases.

This becomes even more serious in the case of subsidized or outsourced projects. The reason for this is that when the payment of subsidies and outsourcing fees from local governments and others is at the end of the fiscal year, expenses must be settled and paid while there is no income. When the timing of expenditures and income differ, it is impossible to continue operations even if they are profitable.

Consider a business with an annual operating budget of 10 million yen during the course of a year that proceeds with its operations while incurring expenses, but the money is paid by the government at the end of the fiscal year after the operations are completed. At this point, if the business has a working capital of 10 million yen, it can proceed with its business while paying its costs; however, if the working capital on hand is small, the business will be short of funds even if it is profitable on its books.

In the case of growing companies, there is the "valley of death" problem, where the expansion of business scale is not accompanied by working capital, and the company goes into bankruptcy. As a result, businesses with small assets cannot apply for large-scale subsidized projects in the first place. For this reason, social businesses cannot grow.

To alleviate these problems, it is important to provide support such as "bridge loans" related to working capital, rather than expanding start-up subsidies. Such support is expected not only from the government, but also from financial institutions, which play a significant role.

2.5.3 *Market Size*

By "market size," we mean the more localized a social business is, the smaller its market size may be. This risk is especially high in regions with declining populations. Hence, businesses in these areas are unable to grow.

The market for social businesses in affected areas is not necessarily large, given that the scope of business is inevitably limited to the region. Meanwhile, if a social business focused on a nationwide social issue could operate in multiple regions, it may be possible to achieve "economies of scale." Specifically, capital investment and bulk purchasing could reduce its costs and, therefore, profit margins could increase.

However, the shopping access problem that arises due to the lack of transportation limits the scope of the business, requires a truck for the mobile supermarket and labor costs. In terms of transportation support, the demand for cab vehicles is also high in each region. The challenge for social businesses in the affected areas is that the limited geographical area makes it difficult to streamline costs, and the market size itself is shrinking because of the declining population. In other words, the business itself is unsustainable because it is unable to secure an adequate market size.

In this regard, while it is problematic to "subsidize" businesses, subsidies and grants are necessary, in order to make business costs more efficient. However, this could be done in other ways, such as capital investment tax incentives for social business operators.

2.6 Conclusion

This chapter reviewed the population situation in affected areas based on census results and the changing political leadership 13 years after the Great East Japan Earthquake. In this context, we examined the challenges in the promotion of business, especially social business, in affected areas, such as the "subsidy trap," the "valley of death," and the "market size problem."

Given that huge budgets have been allocated for reconstruction in the areas affected by the Great East Japan Earthquake, it is important to link "work" and "community development," while changing the approach to subsidies and social business development projects for their most effective use.

One possible change is the "collective impact social business" approach. Here, the government not only provides subsidies and grants, but also designs and promotes projects together with private businesses. In addition, the private sector should collaborate with related businesses in the community to develop projects. Using tourism as an example, it is necessary for the government, tourism associations, local transportation companies, food and beverage companies, and the agriculture and fishery industries to work together to promote tourism projects and ensure their sustainability.

The common element in successful cases is "human resources." In every successful case, there is always a key person, whether a leader or coordinator, whose trust and enthusiasm are the driving force behind the activities. It is precisely this person who fosters social capital, creates a community, and develops it into a collective impact model. Therefore, human resource development is indispensable for fostering social business in affected areas. In particular, it is necessary to develop management personnel and people who can "see the forest for the trees;" in other words, community organizers. Such "investment in people" is important.

Thirteen years after the Great East Japan Earthquake, reconstruction has entered a new stage. This implies that subsidies and social businesses must also change. As the population continues to decline, social business will play a major role in the new "creative reconstruction."

References

Kania, John and Mark Kramer (2011) "Collective Impact," *Stanford Social Innovation Review*.

Kanto Bureau of Economy, Trade and Industry, "Community Business." https://www.kanto.meti.go.jp/seisaku/cb/index.html

Kawachi, Ichiro, S.V. Subramanian and Daniel Kim (2008) *Social Capital and Health*, Springer.

Nakazawa, Katsuyoshi, Shumpei Yaoita and Akira Yokoyama (2016) "Services for Child Care Support as Social Infrastructure: Impact on Birthrate and Migration of Children and Review of Best Practices," *Public Policy Review*, Vol.12, No.1, Policy Research Institute, Ministry of Finance, Japan.

Putnam, Robert D. (1993) *Making Democracy Work: Civic Traditions in Modern Italy*, Princeton University Press.

Putnam, Robert D. (2000) *Bowling Alone: The Collapse and Revival of the American Community*, Simon & Schuster.

Riku Cafe. http://rikucafe.jp/

Statistics Bureau, Ministry of Internal Affairs and Communications (2015) *National Census of 2015*, Japan.

Statistics Bureau, Ministry of Internal Affairs and Communications (2020) *National Census of 2020*, Japan.

Toba, Futoshi (2001) "Looking Back 10 Years after the Great East Japan Earthquake at the Reconstruction Site (Interviewer: Shumpei Yaoita)," Kaikakusha.

Tono City. https://www.city.tono.iwate.jp/index.cfm/4653172296.html

Yunus, Muhammad (2010) *Building Social Business: The New Kind of Capitalism that Serves Humanity's Most Pressing Needs*, Public Affairs.

Yaoita, Shumpei (2017) *Chihou Sousei no Sougouseisakuron*, Keisoshobo.

Yaoita, Shumpei and Miho, Nosaka (2020) "Social Business for Reconstruction," in Keiko Hirono and Yaguchi, Kazuhiro ed. *10 years after the great East Japan earthquake: Analysis of issues in regeneration and development: from the perspectives of economic analysis and mental care*, Taisei Shuppan.

Chapter 3
Urban Development and Town Planning toward Reconstruction

Kazuhiro Yaguchi

Abstract This chapter discusses urban development and town planning following the Great East Japan Earthquake. Considering the declining population and severe fiscal constraints in the affected areas, urban development with compact cities is an effective model. The main analyses in this study are: (1) a microeconomic analysis of the impact of the compact city policy on the land market, and (2) a study of proposed policies to promote a compact city. Microeconomic analysis reveals that compact city policies contribute to more efficient resource allocation if urban externalities are realized. This also demonstrates that public transportation policies are important for promoting compact cities. Thus, I conclude that compact cities and public transportation policies are strategic complements. Furthermore, it is important for the affected areas to have plans that incorporate disaster prevention and mitigation measures. Therefore, establishing a system that passes on the lessons learned from the earthquake to future generations is important.

Keywords Great East Japan Earthquake · Compact city · Urban development · Town planning

3.1 Introduction

Urban development and town planning for reconstruction are important issues for areas affected by the Great East Japan Earthquake. In the short term, the most urgent issue is the restoration of lifelines such as electricity, gas, water, and transportation networks, including roads. Restoration of such social infrastructure is the first step toward recovery. Furthermore, housing-related measures must be implemented

K. Yaguchi (✉)
Faculty of Economics, Keiai University, Chiba-shi, Chiba, Japan
e-mail: k-yaguchi@u-keiai.ac.jp

K. N. Hirono, K. Yaguchi (eds.), *Reconstruction Period and the Stages of Regeneration After a Great Earthquake*, New Frontiers in Regional Science: Asian Perspectives 83, https://doi.org/10.1007/978-981-96-8822-7_3

immediately after an earthquake because housing is the foundation of life. Conversely, in the long term, issues related to urban development and town planning should not be limited to individual aspects such as social infrastructure and housing, but should be viewed as more spatial and sustainable issues.

Generally, urban development and town planning affect not only people's lives but also the socioeconomic conditions of the region. Therefore, urban development and town planning for reconstruction are the most important policy issues for the affected areas. Each affected area has a declining and aging population, a relatively high proportion of primary industries, and a difficult financial situation. These characteristics affect urban development and town planning.

Not limited to the areas affected by the Great East Japan Earthquake, urban development in Japan has been characterized by the expansion of urban areas into the suburbs, focusing on regional development. However, this model fits societies with relatively ample finances and a growing population, as was the case during periods of rapid economic growth, but not now. Therefore, current urban development and town planning will require a model different from the development-centered one, which expands urban areas into the suburbs. Additionally, the Great East Japan Earthquake highlighted the importance of disaster resilience. Post-disaster urban development must incorporate disaster prevention and mitigation mechanisms.

In this chapter, I discuss urban development and town planning for recovery from the Great East Japan Earthquake, keeping in mind the individual areas affected by the disaster. After the *intensive reconstruction period* (FY2011–FY2015), the restoration of social infrastructure and disposal of earthquake debris had already been completed. From this point onward, urban development and town planning aimed at disaster recovery became an issue. To this end, having a firm philosophy and various policies to achieve this goal is important.

3.2 Recommendations for Urban Development and Town Planning

In response to the Great East Japan Earthquake, many experts and practitioners made proposals for urban development and town planning in affected areas, including the government-led Reconstruction Design Council. Additionally, the affected municipalities formulated plans for recovery and reconstruction from the disaster and made references to policies for urban development and town planning.

On June 25, 2011, the Reconstruction Design Council released *Towards Reconstruction "Hope beyond the Disaster"* in response to the Great East Japan Earthquake. This report covers a wide range of areas, including urban development and town planning, livelihood support for disaster victims, regional industrial recovery, and even a review of energy strategies; it has influenced the recovery and reconstruction plans of many affected municipalities.

However, given the timing of its release, this report has more of a grand design and ideal direction for reconstruction than a new set of concrete policy measures. Nonetheless, this report contains important recommendations for the consideration of urban development and town planning issues in the affected areas.

The Reconstruction Design Council's recommendations represent measures to be adopted in terms of software, hardware, and direct (protection) and indirect (evacuation) measures. Hardware and direct measures include the construction of *tsunami breakwaters,*[1] and *coastal dikes.*[2] From this perspective, many coastal municipalities have developed disaster prevention measures. Many coastal municipalities have developed disaster prevention measures, primarily from this perspective. However, recent earthquakes have demonstrated that these measures alone are insufficient. The earthquake destroyed several breakwaters and coastal dikes. The Reconstruction Design Council's proposal is unique in that it emphasizes the perspectives of indirect and direct evacuation.

By contrast, software and indirect measures include disaster prevention education, training, and community planning. This is related to town planning. This report includes recommendations from a broader perspective than disaster prevention and mitigation and refers to urban development and town planning. The recommendations include the following. "Rebuilding the regions must therefore proceed with a view to creating compact towns or villages that also give due consideration to the elderly and the vulnerable, and take into account other factors, including ease of living, landscapes, environment, public transportation, energy conservation and anti-crime measures. Above all, with regard to landscapes, it would be preferable to rebuild the regions that have a sense of unity, based on thorough discussion and consensus among local residents" (Reconstruction Design Council 2011).

The term "compact towns and villages" is used in the proposal, and is connected to the compact city concept that has been attracting attention as an urban development and town planning method. It is also a concept that goes along with the "eco-town" concept advocated by Prime Minister Naoto Kan at the time of the earthquake.

Urban development and town planning for reconstruction, based on the compact city concept, are currently underway. In the coastal areas of Yamamoto-cho, Miyagi Prefecture, and Rikuzentakata-shi, Iwate Prefecture, measures to create a compact city were implemented immediately after the earthquake. Miyagi Prefecture's Basic Plan for Earthquake Reconstruction lists 10 points for reconstruction, one of which is "the formation of eco-towns utilizing renewable energy," which essentially aligns with the compact city concept.

[1] A "tsunami breakwater" refers to a structure that is built in the sea to protect harbors and fishing ports from waves from the open sea and to protect inland areas from tsunamis.

[2] A "coastal dike" refers to a structure built on land (in coastal areas) to protect inland areas from large waves caused by typhoons, tsunamis, and so on.

3.3 Compact City

This section discusses the philosophy and goals of the compact city, which has been the focus of significant attention in urban development and town planning for reconstruction. This study provides an economic and theoretical analysis of policies for promoting a compact city. I conduct an explicit analysis of the urban land market and its impact on resource allocation.

3.3.1 Compact City Philosophy and Goals

A compact city is an urban vision that has been attracting attention in Europe and other developed countries since the early 1990s in response to the global trend toward sustainable development. It is an environmentally symbiotic city in which cities are clustered three-dimensionally to make the space more compact while preserving the natural environment of the surrounding areas. The goals are to revitalize the city center, high-level land use, and energy and resource conservation.

The OECD (2012) identifies the following five reasons why the current situation surrounding cities underscores the need for compact cities: (1) they protect excessive land resource use from advancing urbanization; (2) the global climate change is creating new problems and solutions for cities; (3) rising energy prices are affecting living conditions and transportation costs; (4) the economic crisis is making it difficult to maintain local finances and invest in new infrastructure; and (5) urban policies need to be tailored to the aging of the population.

Mitsuhashi (2016) summarized the significance and effects of compact cities from an urban planning perspective based on the following six points: (1) they reduce fossil fuel consumption by curbing automobile traffic and promoting the use of public transportation; (2) preserve the natural environment and protect agricultural and rural lands in the surrounding areas by curbing urban sprawl; (3) revitalize urban areas through higher density and mixed uses; (4) form and maintain local communities through reduced travel distances; (5) reduce maintenance burdens through the effective use of social infrastructure; and (6) preserve historical and cultural heritage.

All these arguments highlight the significance of compact cities in avoiding excessive land use, considering the environment, reviewing automobile-centered transportation systems, and reducing the burden on public finances by reducing social infrastructure development. Ensuring the sustainability of a city is another key element of the project. The particular importance for the affected areas is the reduction in travel distances described in point (4). As the population in the affected areas is aging, constructing medical facilities such as hospitals is important. Therefore, the construction and guidance of medical facilities in town centers will help shorten travel times.

Additionally, the reduction in the burden of social infrastructure described in point (5) is a financial advantage that is important for local governments in the affected areas. In a compact city, urban functions are concentrated in the center of the city; therefore, social infrastructure development is concentrated in the center. In conventional city planning, which expands urban areas into the suburbs, social infrastructure development must be widely dispersed at the same time as the city expands. In this respect, a compact city has the advantage of saving costs in the construction and maintenance of social infrastructure.

Newman and Kenworthy (1989) used objective indicators to describe a compact city. They defined a compact city by focusing on energy conservation. If gasoline consumption per capita was taken on the vertical axis of a two-dimensional diagram and population density on the horizontal axis, they defined a compact city as one located in the lower right-hand corner of the diagram (see Fig. 3.1.). This indicates that the population density is higher owing to the concentration of urban functions, but gasoline consumption is lower owing to reduced automobile traffic. The cities located in the upper left of the figure are defined as expanded cities. This indicates that towns spread to the suburbs and become more car-dependent. Some European cities are located in the lower right corner, whereas some North American cities are located in the upper left corner.

Another advantage of compact cities is their ability to cope with disaster prevention and mitigation. The central city can be formed as far back as possible from the coast, and the surrounding areas can form natural breakwaters with seawall forests to protect the central district of the city along with man-made breakwaters and coastal dikes. A compact city is also friendly to the elderly. Many of the victims of the 2011 tsunami were elderly people, and it was noticeable that elderly people living in coastal areas were unable to escape. Considering this, it is desirable for the elderly to live in an inner city; however, this will require the development of a compact city where they can live on foot or by bicycle without having to rely on automobiles. If a town is compact, public transportation such as community buses can

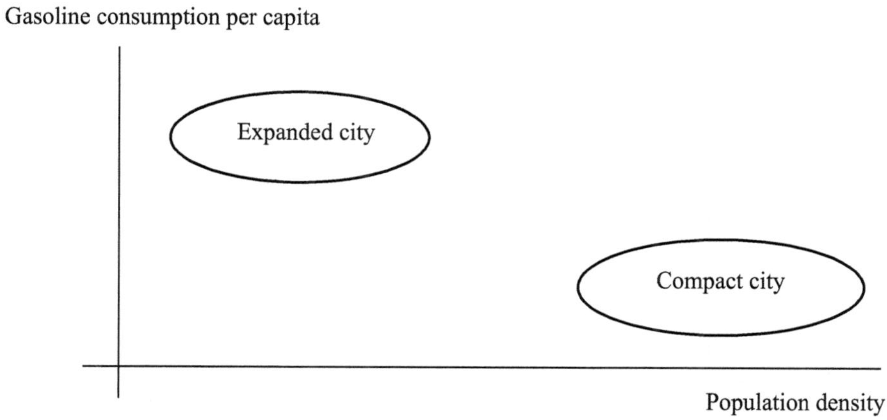

Fig. 3.1 Image of a compact city

easily be developed, and the convenience of the elderly, who are sometimes vulnerable to transportation, will not be lost.

Additionally, the compact city concept is in line with the conventional urban development philosophy and town planning ideas. The attractiveness of compact cities was first demonstrated by Ebenezer Howard's (1889) concept of the garden city. Howard's garden city has a population of approximately 30,000, a well-balanced social stratification, and a self-sufficient population that would live, work, and relax in close proximity. Surrounding such a city is a rural community, and the city is strongly conscious of the connection between urban and rural areas. Furthermore, Jane Jacobs (1961) argued that one of the conditions for a city to have diversity is that city blocks must be short enough to avoid excessive automobile dependence and that people must be densely concentrated enough. The compact city philosophy has a strong affinity with Howard's and Jacobs's ideas.

3.3.2 Impact of Compact Cities on the Land Market

What would be the impact on cities if urban development and town planning based on the compact city philosophy were implemented? Focusing on the urban land market, I analyze the impact from the perspective of resource allocation. A compact city can be divided into a central area where public facilities and urban development take place, and a rural area where environmental preservation is emphasized. Particularly, the mixed use of land, such as the construction of a large shopping center in the peripheral area, is restricted. Zoning regulations must be introduced to enforce these classifications strictly. A partial equilibrium analysis is conducted to determine the impact of these zoning regulations on the land market (see Fig. 3.2.).

In Fig. 3.2, the vertical axis represents the land value, and the horizontal axis represents the land area, where the total land area of a city is expressed as the length of O_1O_2. Two types of land use were distinguished: urban areas (residential,

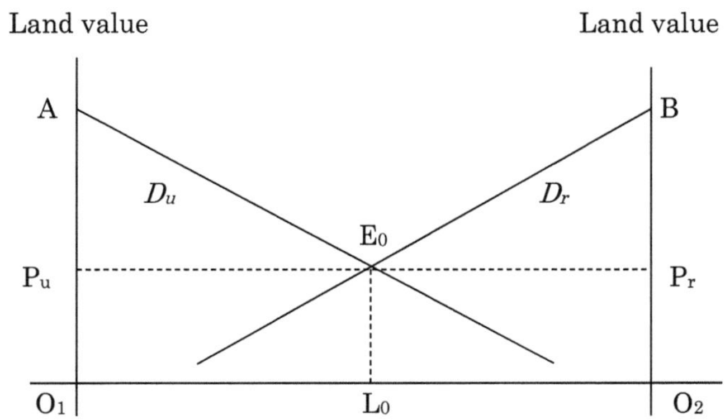

Fig. 3.2 Land market of cities

commercial, and industrial land) and rural areas (unused land, agricultural land, and nature conservation areas). The land in the urban area is taken from O_1 on the left to right, and the land in the rural area is taken from O_2 on the right to left. Here, D_u is the demand curve for land in urban areas and D_r is the demand curve for land in rural areas. The demand curve for land in rural areas is drawn leftward because rural land is moved from O_2 to the left. The market equilibrium is reached at E_0, where the demand curves for both types of land intersect, with O_1L_0 representing the area of land in urban areas and O_2L_0 representing the area of land in rural areas. Here, I analyze the effect of regional development on expanding the suburbs that Japan has undertaken since the end of the 1950s (see Fig. 3.3.).

Figure 3.3 illustrates the effects of regional development, which expands the suburbs. When implemented, the demand for land in urban areas increases. If the urban planning authority relaxes zoning regulations, development will be encouraged. This effect was represented by a rightward shift in the demand curve for land in urban areas from Du to Du. The demand for land in rural areas is assumed to be constant. Consequently, O_1L' is the land area in urban areas, O_2L' is the land area in rural areas, and the land area in urban areas expands. This figure depicts regional development that has expanded the urban area into the suburbs.

Next, I analyze the effect of the compact city policy aimed at creating a compact city. E' in Fig. 3.4 is the same as E' in Fig. 3.3, and is the market equilibrium before the implementation of the policy, where the development site has expanded to the suburbs (see Fig. 3.4.).

Compact city policies must implement zoning to concentrate urban functions in the city center. To this end, policies have been implemented to reduce urban land areas. Specific policy instruments include strengthening the zoning regulations and prohibiting development. These policies have two main effects.

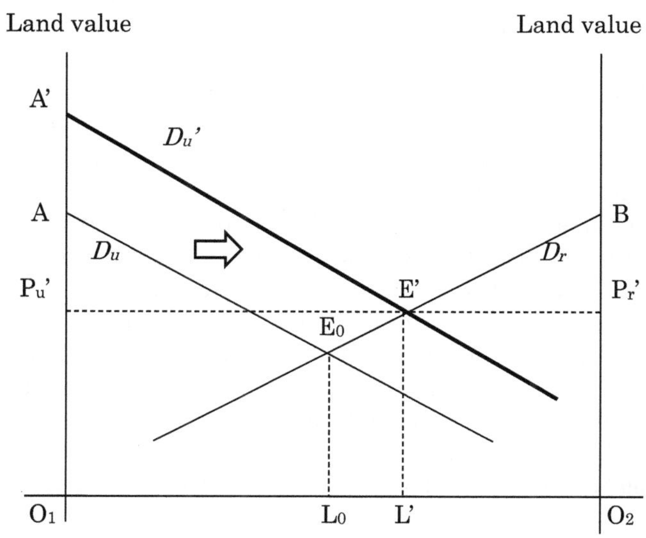

Fig. 3.3 Effects of regional development

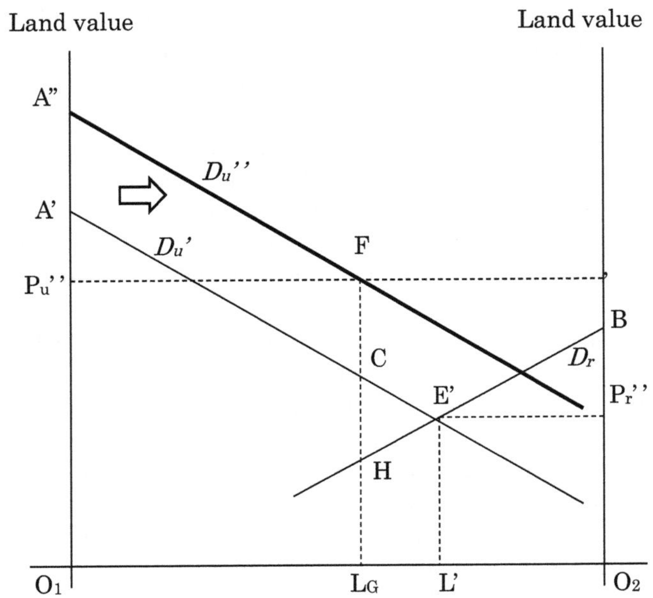

Fig. 3.4 Effects of the compact city policy

The first is a reduction in the urban land area. This is achieved by regulating L as a policy instrument in which the urban planning authority determines the percentage of land to be used. The second is the external economies of agglomeration, in which a reduction in the area of urban land leads to higher use of the central district, which in turn revitalizes the central district and increases productivity, and the economies of density, in which the concentration of various firms and urban functions at high densities lowers transaction costs. Both these effects represent the external economy of a city. When these effects occur, the demand for land in urban areas increases. However, external economic effects are hypothetical, and whether they actually occur must be examined through empirical analysis. One of the advantages of a compact city is its ability to concentrate urban functions at its center. External economic effects are also considered.

The city planning authority moves and fixes L to L_G to shrink developed land to form a compact city. The city's external economic effects then shifted the demand curve for developed land from Du' to Du''. Consequently, the urban land area shrinks from O_1L' to O_1L_G, whereas the rural land area expands from O_2L' to O_2L_G. The land price in the urban area becomes Pu''and that in the rural area becomes Pr'', and the land prices in the two areas are at different levels. When land prices are at different levels, land in rural areas with lower land prices will be purchased when there are no regulations; however, this will not occur if the zoning regulations and development control measures are binding.

Furthermore, I analyze the impact of the compact city policy on resource allocation. To evaluate the policy, I compare the surplus before and after implementation.

Given that the market equilibrium before policy implementation is represented in Fig. 3.3 and that after policy implementation in Fig. 3.4, the total surplus in the land market before policy implementation is O_1A'E' BO_2 in size. The breakdown is as follows: Triangle A'E'Pu′ is the consumer surplus of the consumers of the land of urban area and square O_1Pu'E'L' is the surplus of its land owners. Triangle BE'Pr′ is the consumer surplus of land of rural area demanders and square O_2Pr'E'L' is the surplus of their land owners.

The total surplus in the land market after the policy is implemented is the size of O_1A' 'F LG, the surplus of land of urban area, plus O_2BHL_G, the surplus of land of rural area. Comparing before and after the implementation of the policy, the policy increases the surplus by the size of parallelogram A'A' 'FC, but decreases the surplus by the size of triangle E'CH. Therefore, the impact of policy on resource allocation has not yet been theoretically determined. To determine the exact impact, it is necessary to confirm the magnitude of parallelogram A'A' 'FC and triangle E'CH through empirical analysis.

Therefore, if the external economic effects of high-level use of central districts do not emerge, the policy will distort land-use allocation and lead to inefficiencies in resource allocation. In this sense, the evaluation of compact city policies depends on the magnitude of the city's external economies. If realized, a compact city policy will prove to be desirable in terms of resource allocation.

In addition, when evaluated from a distributional perspective, the compact city policy only increases the consumer surplus of area of rural land demanders. The size of the surplus of other rural landowners and the demanders and owners of the urban land area is not determined before and after the policy. This indicates that a compact city policy will certainly benefit rural land users. However, the benefits to other economic entities are indeterminable.

3.4 Attitudes of Residents in the Affected Areas

Although economic theoretical analysis has shown the effectiveness of compact city policies, what is important in this case is whether the residents support compact cities. If residents return to the pre-disaster state, it will be difficult to gain an understanding of urban development and town planning for a compact city.

Additionally, the Great East Japan Earthquake made people realize the threat of tsunamis. It is particularly important to consider tsunami countermeasures in coastal areas. Coastal dikes have been discussed in this regard. In the aforementioned "Image of Measures Related to Tsunami Disaster Prevention Community and Town planning" presented by the Reconstruction Design Council in response to the Great East Japan Earthquake, the construction of coastal dikes is listed as a difficult and direct measure and is highly important. However, residents do not necessarily fully support the construction of coastal dikes. To confirm these points, this section describes the results of an attitude survey of residents in affected areas.

3.4.1 Attitudes Toward Town Scale

The first question I address is whether to aim for a town that is the same size as before the earthquake or a town that is the right size for the actual conditions of the disaster area. A town of a size appropriate for the actual situation of the affected area is a more compact town that accepts the declining population.

Since the 2011 earthquake, the population has continued to flow out of the coastal areas of the affected areas. Combined with financial constraints, maintaining the existing size of the city has become difficult. This, in turn, affects the ability to convince residents of a compact city to be a model for urban development.

What do residents of the affected areas think about the scale of their towns? Figure 3.5 shows the results of a survey asking whether they would like their towns to be the same size as before the disaster (a) or whether they would like their towns to be of a different size from before the disaster but still appropriate to their actual situation (b) (see Fig. 3.5.).

In the three prefectures affected by the disaster, 13.7% of the respondents (including more like "a") said that they would keep the same size of the town as before the disaster. Conversely, 85.7% of the respondents (including more like "b") said that they would make the town the same size as it was before the disaster, but more appropriate to the actual situation. Thus, more than 80% of residents in disaster-affected areas are oriented toward town planning that fits the current situation in the region, which is consistent with the promotion of compact cities.

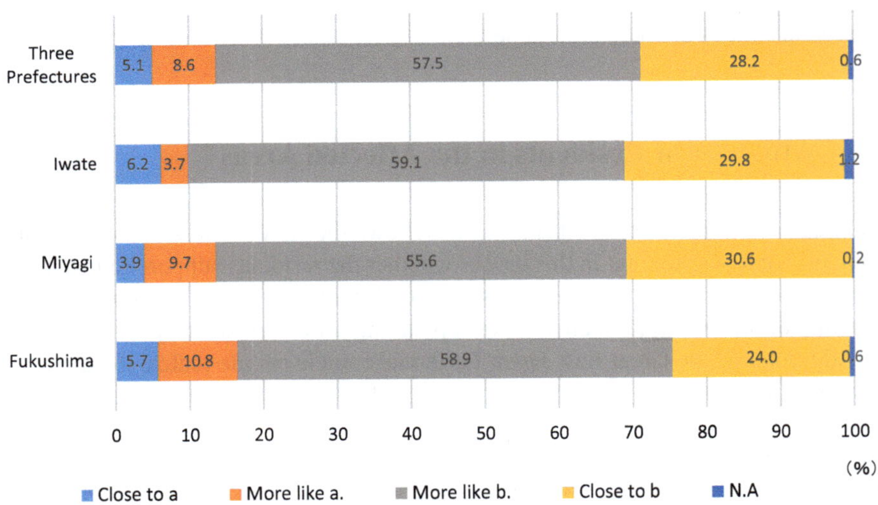

Fig. 3.5 Attitude toward town scale. Note 1: Survey period: December 12–20, 2015. Note 2: Number of valid responses: 1368 people in the three affected prefectures, 324 in Iwate, 588 in Miyagi, and 456 in Fukushima. Note 3: Choice "a" is for "make the town the same size as before the disaster," and choice "b" is for "make the town suitable for the actual situation even if the size changes from before the disaster. Source: Prepared by the author based on Kono et al. (2016)

Looking at the three prefectures affected by the prefecture, Iwate, Miyagi, and Fukushima prefectures, in that order, clearly have the most opinions toward town planning suited to the actual conditions of the region. This may indicate the size of the original town and the extent of damage caused by the earthquake, and simultaneously, it may also depend on the extent of damage. In Fukushima Prefecture, in particular, the accident at the Fukushima Daiichi Nuclear Power Plant seems to have had an impact, as well as the damage caused by the tsunami. The fact that people were forced to evacuate their towns because of the accident, which was probably a man-made disaster, seems to indicate a strong will to return to their original towns and villages.

3.4.2 *Attitudes Toward Coastal Dikes*

Next, I examine awareness of coastal dikes. *Level 1 coastal dikes* are those that can withstand tsunamis that occur once every hundred years and have the capacity to protect human lives, property, and economic activities.[3] The opinions regarding *Level 1 coastal dikes* are as follows (see Fig. 3.6.).

Figure 3.6 shows that 63.5% of the respondents in the three affected prefectures were in favor of the construction of *Level 1 coastal dikes* (including those close to

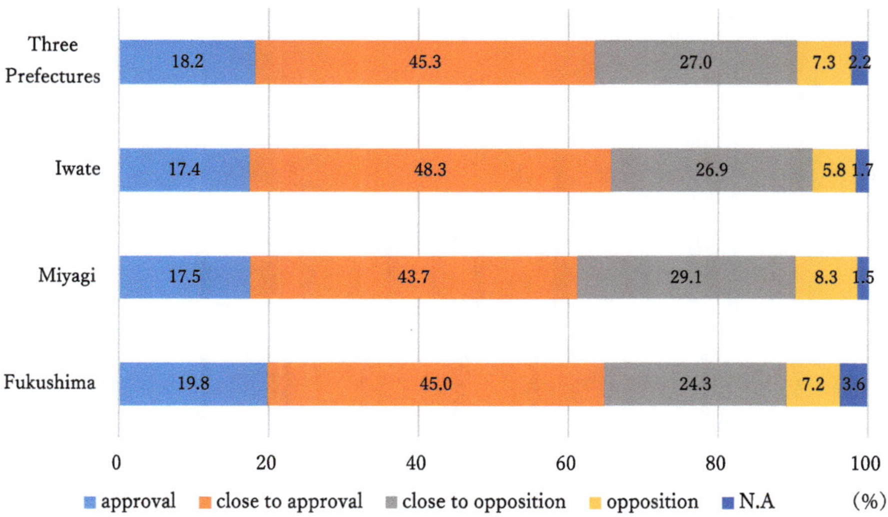

Fig. 3.6 Attitude toward Level 1 costal dikes. Note: The survey period and number of valid responses are the same as in Fig. 3.5. Source: Prepared by the author based on Kono et al. (2016)

[3] *Level 2 coastal dikes* are even larger than Level 1 dikes. This is based on the assumption that a tsunami occurs once every 1000 years or so. In addition to protecting human lives, these levees meet disaster-mitigation performance requirements such as reducing economic losses, preventing major secondary disasters, and enabling early restoration.

approval), whereas 34.3% were opposed (including those close to opposition). Of the three prefectures, Miyagi Prefecture had a slightly higher percentage of those opposed to the plan than the other two.

In Miyagi Prefecture, Governor Yoshihiro Murai has shown a positive attitude toward the construction of tsunami breakwaters and coastal dikes. However, in some parts of Miyagi Prefecture, residents do not always agree. Figure 3.7 shows the reasons for the opposition to coastal dikes (see Fig. 3.7.).

The most frequently cited reason for opposition in the three affected prefectures was that "we should not rely on coastal dikes alone," followed by "we cannot handle tsunamis that exceed our expectations." The massive tsunami generated by the earthquake advanced inland, destroying several breakwaters and coastal dikes. It is assumed that this is the reason for the opposition. These responses were followed by the construction and maintenance costs. Given the severe financial situation of local governments in affected areas, cost constraints cannot be ignored, and it has been confirmed that even a certain percentage of residents in the affected areas have a sense of cost.

In addition, a certain number of respondents gave the following reasons: "We might be caught off guard and late to escape" and "We won't know when a tsunami will occur." Another problem is that high coastal dikes would block the sea and

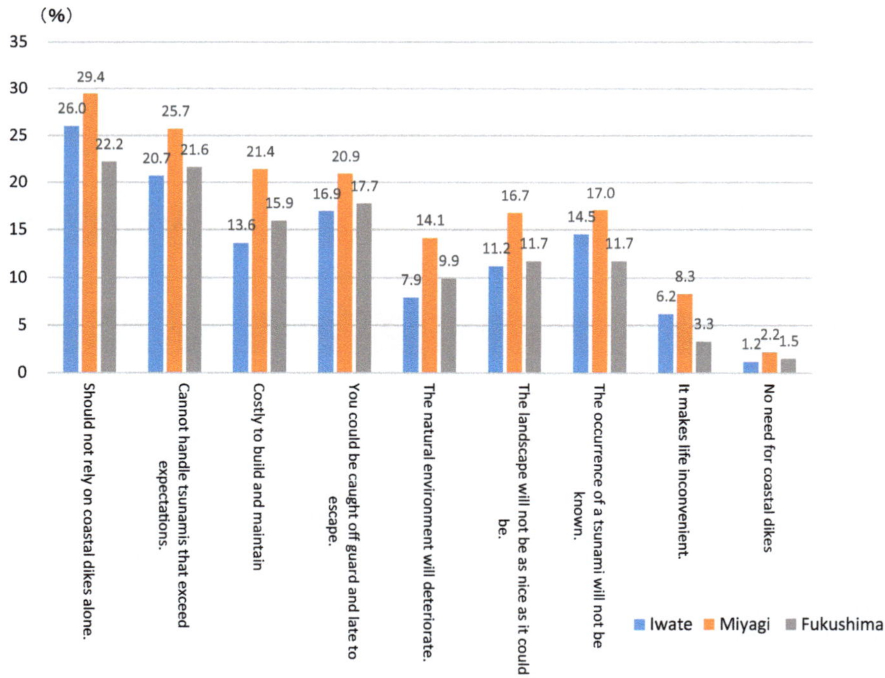

Fig. 3.7 Reasons for opposing the construction of coastal dikes (multiple responses). Note: The number of valid responses is the sum of those who answered "opposition" and "close to opposition" in Fig. 3.6. Source: Prepared by the author based on Kono et al. (2016)

obstruct visibility, thus delaying discovery of the tsunami's arrival. These opinions suggest the limitation of relying solely on coastal dikes for tsunami countermeasures. Some of the opinions against the construction include "the natural environment will deteriorate" and "the landscape will not be as nice as it could be." Although the sea along the *Sanriku coast* brings with it a fear of tsunamis, it is usually a rich natural blessing and an important resource for the region. The sea is also a source of livelihood for fishermen. For this reason, local people try to live as close as possible to the sea. Even after an earthquake, the opposing coastal dikes may reflect the regional characteristics of the *Sanriku coastal area*.

Thus, there is no complete support for the reliance on coastal dikes for tsunami protection. In fact, in some areas of Miyagi Prefecture, residents voiced opposition and doubts regarding the construction of coastal dikes. However, some towns and villages in Iwate Prefecture expressed the opinion that the height of the embankments proposed by the prefecture was too low.

Coastal dikes are public goods. This is because they provide safety services against tsunamis to a wide range of residents. However, the existence of a coastal dike itself can be an obstacle to fisheries and tourism because it ruins the landscape and natural environment, and can also have a negative impact because it blocks the view of the sea, making people unaware of the arrival of a tsunami. These negative impacts are opportunity costs because they do not result in monetary payments.[4] Residents are aware of the meaning of opportunity costs even if they do not know the term; however, the government is unaware of it because there is no payment. The discussion on coastal dikes was confusing because residents and the government did not share the same awareness of this negative aspect.

3.5 Urban Development and Town Planning Issues

This section discusses future urban development and town planning issues in disaster-affected areas and policies to promote compact cities based on previous studies.[5] The issues to be discussed include land use, public transportation policies complementary to compact city policies, and the transmission of earthquake experience to future generations.

[4] Nagamine (2013) discusses the issues related to seawall maintenance in terms of benefits and costs. The costs include not only financial payments such as construction and maintenance costs, but also opportunity costs, which are invisible costs.

[5] The following discussion is based on and expanded upon Yaguchi (2011) and Yaguchi (2020).

3.5.1 Land Use

As suggested by the economic theory analysis in Sect. 3.3, thorough zoning is essential for a compact city policy to become viable. This is because external economic effects can be expected because of this policy. If zoning works, the external economic effects of the advanced use of the city center will be realized, and the total surplus will increase. The financial burden will be reduced through the intensive installation of urban social infrastructure such as public facilities. If unregulated development that ignores zoning is allowed, it will only lead back to a traditional diffuse suburban town.

Through empirical analysis, Kutsuzawa et al. (2018) confirmed that cities become more compact when the urbanized area per resident is smaller. This shows that thorough zoning is effective in forming compact cities. The promotion of compact cities requires the purification of land use, which also applies to surrounding areas. However, this is not sufficient to allow development in the periphery. If unused land is allowed to continue unabated, inefficiencies in land use will occur, and the area will eventually be subjected to the pressures of development. The periphery should be used as farmland or nature conservation land. If it remains as unused land awaiting development, it simply reverts to its original state.

An example from Portland, U.S.A. provides an example in this regard. Portland is well-known as an advanced compact city and has implemented an Urban Growth Boundary (UGB) to regulate urban development on its periphery. Yoshida (2013) described the effects of the UGB as a policy to promote the development of farmland on the periphery. It understands this effect as an upward shift in the agricultural land rent curve based on a partial equilibrium analysis, which he points out is effective in promoting compact cities. Portland has provided tax breaks for prime farmlands and strengthened urban-rural linkages. Since the introduction of the UGB, Portland has witnessed an increase in sales for farmers and ranchers.

However, this does not mean that implementing farmland policies in Japan will be sufficient. Even now, farmland taxation has been reduced and there is a problem of low agricultural productivity in Japan. Considering this, considering how land should be used in the surrounding areas, as well as revitalizing the central area, is necessary. Other than agriculture, one example is the use of land for solar power generation and tsunami protection.

A further policy could be for municipalities to lease land from landowners near coastlines. The idea is to build public and disaster prevention facilities on rented land and encourage landowners near the coastline to move to the city center. It is important for the municipality to sign the contract from the beginning for the long term with a view to renewing the contract, but for the landowner, the result will be the same as when leasing the land held near the coastline to a stable tenant. This is an advantage for the landowner over continuing to hold the land. The decline in real estate prices in the suburbs is often raised as an argument against promoting compact cities; however, for affected areas, the question is how to develop coastal areas away from the center of the city in a non-residential manner.

3.5.2 *Public Transportation Policy*

Public transportation must be improved for compact cities to function realistically. Affected areas have traditionally been car-dependent; however, as the population ages, an increasing number of people are becoming unable to travel by car. In reality, in affected areas, those who can move freely by car coexist with those who are less able to use public transportation. Although some have argued for the importance of developing railroads in this regard, there are limitations as well. Therefore, it is necessary to actively promote Bus Rapid Transit (BRT) systems, which have been introduced in affected areas.

It is not a question of which comes first, compact city or public transportation policy, but both need to be promoted. If only compact city policies other than public transportation policies are promoted, it will lead to urban development that lacks convenience in mobility and will cause excessive use of automobiles in the city center, which will have an environmental impact. Conversely, if public transportation policies alone are prioritized, this will have the opposite effect on a compact city, as it will increase the distance that residents can travel by choosing new transportation networks. Compact city and public transportation policies are strategic complements. Some studies have shown that a decline in private car use has a significant impact on urban compactness (e.g., Kutsuzawa et al. 2018), suggesting that improving public transportation is an important part of a compact city policy. Additionally, as urban functions are concentrated in the center of a compact city, increased car use should be avoided if environmental considerations are prioritized in the center of a compact city.

Given the increasing elderly population, public transportation has become an increasingly important issue. Generally, elderly people are more vulnerable to traffic congestion, and the number of elderly people who voluntarily return their driver's licenses is expected to increase. In relatively small towns and villages, the use of community buses as a more accessible means of transportation may also be effective.

3.5.3 *Passing down the Legacy of the Earthquake*

The earthquake brought about various effects, such as the collapse of buildings, destruction of social infrastructure, and other physical damage, as well as a burden on the human spirit. This is the problem with passing on lessons learned from the earthquake. In urban development and town planning for reconstruction, passing on lessons learned from the earthquake to the next generation must also be considered. Particularly, the transmission of lessons from earthquakes is an important issue in terms of preparing for major earthquakes, such as those in the *Nankai Trough*, which are expected to occur in the not-too-distant future with a high probability of occurrence.[6]

Japan is prone to earthquakes, and the area facing the *Sanriku coast*, which was hit by the Great East Japan Earthquake, has been affected by tsunamis many times before. There have been cases in which lessons learned from past tsunami disasters have been applied to minimize damage. A typical example is the long-standing folklore of "*Tsunami Tendenko*" in Kamaishi City, Iwate Prefecture.[7]

Kamaishi took advantage of this tradition by introducing it into evacuation drills at elementary and junior high schools. Consequently, on the day of the earthquake, approximately 3000 students from elementary and junior high schools in Kamaishi City immediately evacuated, resulting in a survival rate of 99.8%. This event is called *Kamaishi no kiseki (Kamaishi miracle).* Disaster prevention education and training were also identified as important measures by the Reconstruction Design Council (2011), and such a perspective should be introduced into education policies.

Facilities such as reference libraries have been developed in buildings, displaying panels showing the damage caused by the earthquake and video footage of what it was like at the time of the disaster. Additionally, some buildings damaged by the earthquake were preserved in their original form. Such buildings allow the horror of the earthquake and the wisdom of how to prepare for it to be used as lessons for future generations. Government-supported prayer parks were constructed in the Iwate, Miyagi, and Fukushima prefectures.

Additionally, the Great East Japan Earthquake was also a nuclear disaster, conveying the fear of nuclear disasters to future generations. It is necessary to establish a system to convey the true nature of a nuclear disaster, from its beginning to the response immediately after the accident, to the evacuation of local residents, and so on. In doing so, it is desirable to introduce the reality of the nuclear disaster and convey it to the next generation, rather than denouncing a particular group or ideology.[8]

3.6 Conclusion

The Great East Japan Earthquake caused the horrors of natural disasters to become evident. Therefore, the perspective of disaster prevention and mitigation is indispensable for urban development and town planning. Compact cities can serve as

[6] Nemoto and Yaguchi (2021), based on field research, focus their discussion on the significance of earthquake lore and specific lore facilities.

[7] *Tendenko* is a word that means "individual." It is a saying that when you feel a big tremor at the seashore, you should run to high ground as quickly as possible to save your own life, regardless of your relatives, because a tsunami is coming.

[8] The *Commutan Fukushima* (Miharu-cho, Tamura-gun, Fukushima Prefecture) and the *Great East Japan Earthquake and Nuclear Disaster Lore Museum* (Futaba-cho, Futaba-gun, Fukushima Prefecture) are two such facilities that convey the experience of the nuclear disaster.

effective models for the reconstruction of affected areas. Particularly, the high aging rate of the population in affected areas calls for urban development that does not impose a heavy burden on transportation.

Thus, compact cities should not be viewed as economic policy instruments for revitalizing central city areas. The goal of revitalizing central city areas requires a policy instrument for the local economy, and forcibly linking local economic revitalization with urban development issues is not necessary. The primary goals of residential safety, comfort, and convenience are essential for urban development and town planning during earthquake recovery.

What is required to actively promote community development in accordance with the concept of a compact city? Although financial inducements through taxation and subsidies may be necessary, building an understanding and consensus among local residents regarding compact cities is also important. Many of the affected areas are rich in natural environments. Therefore, from the perspective of preserving the natural environment, there is little incentive to promote compact cities. Under such circumstances, forcibly promoting a compact city may only be perceived as a disruption to the local community because of forced resettlement. As shown in the results of the awareness survey in Sect. 3.4, it was easy to obtain residents' agreement to promote compact cities in the affected areas. It is important for the formation of a compact city to maintain the perspective of a safe and secure lifestyle, rather than revitalizing the local economy.

Another challenge in reconstruction is passing on the experience of the Great East Japan Earthquake to future generations. This requires a steady stream of disaster education. Through such steady activities, the horror of the earthquake and the lessons learned from it will not fade away, but can be utilized to prepare for the next disaster. Solid handed-down activities are an effective means of creating a culture of disaster prevention. The establishment of a culture of disaster prevention in individual communities provides meaningful social capital for urban development and town planning for reconstruction.

References

Howard E (1889) *Garden cities of tomorrow*, Town and Country Planning Association.

Jacobs J (1961) *The death and life of great American cities*, Vintage Books.

Kono K et al (2016) "Five years after the earthquake: public and disaster area attitudes: from the public opinion poll on disaster prevention and energy, *2015," Housou Kenkyu to Chousa (Broadcasting Research and Survey)*, 28–70 (in Japanese).

Kutsuzawa T et al (2018) "The influence of land use regulations on urban compactness," *Keikaku Gyousei (Planning Administration)*, 41(4):38–46 (in Japanese).

Mitsuhashi H (2016) "Compact City-Rinen to Case". In Maruo N et al (eds) *ECOcity–Kankyo City Compact City Fukushi City no Jitsugennimukete,* Tokyo Chuo Keizaisya, 109–130 (in Japanese).

Nagamine J (2013) "A consideration of the law system, cost and benefit, and consensus buildingover a seawall," *Kokyo Sentaku (Public Choice Studies)* 59:143–161 (in Japanese).

Nemoto,T and K.Yaguchi (2021) "Network to transmit lessons from the great East Japanearthquake," *Keikaku Gyousei (Planning Administration)* 44(3):21–26 (in Japanese).
Newman P, Kenworthy J (1989) *Cities and automobile dependence: An international source-book*, Gower.
OECD (2012) *Compact cities policies: a comparative assessment*, OECD Publishing.
Reconstruction Design Council in response to the Great East Japan Earthquake (2011) *Towards Reconstruction, Hope beyond the Disaster*, Report to the Prime Minister of the reconstruction design council in response to the Great East Japan Earthquake.
Yaguchi K (2011) "Jikanjiku wo Kihon ni sueta Futsukousaku wo," *Kaikakusha* 38–41 (in Japanese).
Yaguchi K (2020) "Shinsaigo no Toshi no Seibi to Machidukuri". In Hirono K.N. and K.Yaguchi ed., *Higashinihondaishinsai kara 10 Nen: Saisei Hatten ni Okeru Kadai no Bunseki (Analysis on reconstruction period and the stages of regeneration after a Great Earthquake: Ten Years after Great East Japan Earthquake)*, Tokyo, Taisei Shuppan, 65–84 (in Japanese).
Yoshida Y (2013) "Policy implication from cases in foreign countries for realizing compact cities," *Keikaku Gyousei (Planning Administration)* 36(4):15–20 (in Japanese).

Chapter 4
Earthquake Disaster and Alcohol-Related Problems

Maiko Wakabayashi

Abstract Alcohol-related problems caused by increased drinking among disaster victims due to a sense of loss and a lack of a place to go became an issue after the Great Hanshin-Awaji Earthquake drew attention to the problem. In the Great East Japan Earthquake, despite the early efforts of various support organizations, the reality is that the amount of alcohol consumption increased, and problems related to alcohol consumption occurred in Iwate, Miyagi, and Fukushima, which were severely affected by the disaster. In this study, we conducted interviews with supporters and members of self-help groups and researched materials in order to obtain knowledge that can be applied to the field from the perspective of dealing with alcohol-related problems and the practices and experiences of various organizations. As a result, many supporters realized changes in local responses to alcohol-related problems because of various efforts. However, it was suggested that the welfare issues of the community itself and the fragmentation of the relationships necessary for the support committee due to the impact of COVID-19 are issues for the future.

Keywords Great East Japan Earthquake · Alcohol-Related Problems · Mental Health Care · Disaster Support

4.1 Introduction

Alcohol-related problems during disasters have been considered an issue since the Great Hanshin-Awaji Earthquake drew attention to the problem, and the Sendai City Mental Health Care Team issued a call for people to "be careful not to drink too much alcohol" at evacuation centers on the third day after the earthquake (Okazaki

M. Wakabayashi (✉)
Faculty of Human Welfare, Tokyo Online University, Tokyo, Japan
e-mail: wakabayashi.maiko@internet.ac.jp

K. N. Hirono, K. Yaguchi (eds.), *Reconstruction Period and the Stages of Regeneration After a Great Earthquake*, New Frontiers in Regional Science: Asian Perspectives 83, https://doi.org/10.1007/978-981-96-8822-7_4

(2014)). In addition, the Center for Comprehensive Suicide Prevention and Countermeasures posted "Do not include alcohol in relief supplies to evacuation centers" on its then website[1] on April 11, 2011 (2011), 1 month after the earthquake. In reality, however, the record of the Miyagi Association of Mental Health and Welfare Professionals states that "alcohol drinking at the meeting halls starts in the daytime." (Kimura (2014)).

One of the problems unique to the disaster-affected areas is the physical proximity of "living spaces" in evacuation centers and temporary housing (temporary housing is built in a row-house style, and evacuation centers are not separated by households in the first place). This makes the living spaces of disaster victims closer to each other), which makes it easier for nuisances caused by the above-mentioned problems to occur and become visible to people other than the family members involved. For example, trouble may occur due to verbal abuse caused by intoxication, and neighbors may suffer inconvenience in the form of scattered garbage and odors due to the inability to take care of their own personal belongings.

Furthermore, those around them are swept away and exhausted by the verbal violence caused by the onset of psychiatric symptoms of alcoholism that develop as a result of heavy and continuous drinking, as well as by the lifestyle and health problems caused by heavy drinking. However, because impairment of alcohol intake control is the primary symptom and this is intractable, it is not easy for the person concerned to stop drinking. Alcoholism has been associated with many deaths due to its difficulty in intervention and cure.

Among the various problems occurring in the affected areas, problems in the field of mental health and welfare emerged some time after the disaster and lasted for a long period of time. The alcohol-related problems discussed in this chapter are among the issues that need to be addressed now, 7 years after the disaster.

The flow of this chapter will first provide an overview of alcohol-related problems, with a focus on alcoholism, in order to understand the premise, and then describe the situation in the affected areas.

4.2 Alcohol-Related Problems

4.2.1 What Are Alcohol-Related Problems?

Alcohol-related problems are all alcohol-related problems. This includes not only health problems but also social problems. They affect not only the person who drinks, but also the family and the people around him or her.

---

[1] "Prealcoholism" refers to the interval between normal drinking and dependence. However, this term is new, and in the past, it was called by each of several diagnostic criteria for psychiatric disorders, such as "alcohol abuse" and "harmful use. The Information Evaluation Committee of the Ministry of Health, Labor, and Welfare's e-Health Net website has proposed the term "pre-alcoholism" as a unified term. This document follows suit.

Alcohol-related problems are diverse. In terms of health, there are physical effects (organ damage, trauma, etc.) and mental effects (addiction, depression, suicide, dementia), while in terms of daily life, problems caused by drinking at work can lead to unemployment, unemployment, and poverty due to the cost of alcohol consumption. In terms of the impact on those around them, domestic violence, abuse, and alcohol harassment (e.g., forced drinking) are cited, and in terms of social impact, drunk driving, decreased productivity, and increased medical costs are cited. According to statistics from the Ministry of Health, Labor and Welfare's research group, the social loss caused by excessive alcohol consumption, including all of the above, is estimated to be 4148.3 billion yen.

Alcoholism is a disease caused by continuous heavy drinking, and the distribution of drinking behavior is said to be in three stages: (1) normal drinking, (2) prealcoholism[1], and (3) alcohol dependence. The operational boundary between "prealcoholism" and "alcoholism" is the absence of both withdrawal symptoms[2] and the experience of continuous drinking.[3]

4.2.2 *What Is Alcoholism?*

Alcohol is a psychoactive substance (a substance that affects mental functions such as cognition and emotion). Some psychoactive substances cannot be stopped by one's will once they are used (psychodependence), and when they are constantly present in the body, a tolerance is formed and the "intoxicating" effects such as altered perception are no longer obtained. This leads to a vicious cycle of ever-increasing intake, and as a result of large amounts of continuous intake, adverse biological effects and the involvement of others due to the development of life problems and psychiatric symptoms occur (Japan Association of Training Schools for Mental Health Professionals (2016)).

The biological process leading to alcoholism is described above, but the actual symptoms of alcoholism are broadly defined as a loss of control over drinking. In other words, the "inability to quit" is itself a symptom. Moreover, current medical science has not developed treatment methods to help alcoholics regain control over their drinking. Therefore, to say that "you can stop if you have a strong will" is tantamount to saying that the main symptom should be cured by force of will. The inability to stop is the primary symptom, but there is no way to cure it.

So, is it impossible to reintegrate into society after suffering from alcoholism? It is possible to stop the vicious cycle by continuing to abstain from alcohol. And by

---

[2] Withdrawal symptoms are a syndrome consisting of various symptoms and severity caused by complete or incomplete withdrawal from a substance after repeated and prolonged heavy use of the substance, which may include convulsions, delirium tremens, sleep disorders, and depression.

[3] Continuous drinking is the epitome of uncontrolled drinking, in which alcohol is consumed every few hours and is constantly present in the body for several days or months, during which time food is rarely consumed.

continuing to abstain from alcohol, the alcoholic will be able to lead a social life that is seemingly no different from that of a normal adult. For this reason, support for the prognosis of alcoholics is not aimed at "cure" but at "recovery.

However, some may wonder how a person can recover when impaired control is the main symptom. In fact, the prognosis for treatment of alcoholism is not high, and the sobriety rate of alcoholics is around 30% 1 year after discharge from a medical institution specializing in alcoholism (Higuchi (2007)). In addition, the average life expectancy of alcoholics who die as a result of drinking is reported to be 50–52 years (Ino et al. 1991, Noda et al.1988). However, even this is far better than in the past, when medical care was spoon-fed alcoholism until the first "recovering" person appeared. It was not until the ninth edition of the International Classification of Diseases (ICD-9) in 1979 that alcoholism came to be recognized as a disease on a global scale. The fact that "inability to stop drinking" was a "disease" was not recognized even in the medical world.

Even more troubling is the fact that it is not only society that "refuses to acknowledge" alcoholism, but also the person affected. In particular, the situation in which the individual does not admit to alcoholism is known as "denial," and has been a major obstacle to intervention. For this reason, there is a great deal of interest in denial among supporters, and a variety of findings have emerged, but most of them define denial from the onset of the addiction problem to the point of refusing to acknowledge the loss of control as "primary denial," and denial in the face of the cause of the addiction and its impact on the surroundings as "secondary denial.[4] Psychological recovery is then a process of disengaging this denial at the person's own rocking pace.

4.2.3 "Recovery" and Self-Help Groups

In this context, it is said that the first "recovering" alcoholic was Alcoholics Anonymous (AA), a self-help group established in the United States in 1935 (Noguchi (1996), etc.). Since then, the role of self-help groups in the treatment of alcoholics has been emphasized. In Japan, AAs have been reconstituted as "AA associations" (currently the All Japan Alcoholics Anonymous is the largest organization of AAs in Japan) to fit into the Japanese culture, and are the largest self-help groups for alcoholics in Japan.

[4] Some believe that there are three levels of denial (Yamamoto (2015)). According to this theory, there are three types of denial: "first denial" in which the person does not admit to having an addiction problem; "second denial" in which the person admits to having a problem but does not admit to being out of control because they can stop by themselves; and "third denial" in which the person admits to being out of control but does not explain why addiction became necessary or how much they were harmed by their continued use of addiction. The "third denial" is the one in which the addict does not acknowledge the loss of control because he or she can stop the addiction on their own, and does not bother about why the addiction became necessary or how much trouble they caused to others and how much harm they did to themselves by continuing the addiction.

A self-help group is simply defined as "a group of individuals and their families who have some problems" (Kubo 2004). It is "a voluntary and proactive human service organization with independence and continuity that operates, organizes, and manages itself by utilizing experience and experiential knowledge to generate and promote self-help among its members" (Iwata 2010). The basis of self-help groups is meetings. The rule is not to slander or defame each other during meetings, but in self-help groups for addiction, not limited to alcohol, it is especially important to emphasize "saying and listening" and to tell your own story and listen to the stories of your peers in meetings that are a "safe place" where no one can give you opinions or condemn you. is considered important. The common function of self-help groups is to gain strength for self-determination and social communication, based on the sharing of experiences and self-affirmation, etc. The functions of self-help groups for alcoholics include "the replacement function of the role played by alcohol (reduction of drinking machines, healing of emotions and (reduction of drinking machines, emotional healing, replenishment of energy)" and "the function of creating a new way of life without alcohol (growth of interpersonal skills, rediscovery of self, coping with stigma)" (Noguchi 1996).

Of course, this is not to say that until the present day there has been nothing done by advocates; there are interventions outside of self-help groups to aid in recovery. Motivational interviewing and motivational support, family therapy, psychoeducational programs, behavioral therapy, cognitive-behavioral therapy, and many other programs are available. However, advocates also emphasize the power of self-help groups, which produced the world's first recovering addicts, and the recognition that self-help groups are central to recovery from addiction is evident in the fact that participation in self-help groups is built into alcohol rehabilitation programs across the country. This is evidenced by the fact that participation in self-help groups is incorporated into alcohol rehabilitation programs throughout the country.

4.3 Disasters and Alcoholism

Although there is a wealth of knowledge on alcohol-related problems, including post-disaster alcoholism, both in Japan and abroad, there are few findings that clearly show an increase in alcoholism due to disasters because it is difficult to determine the amount of alcohol consumed before a disaster (Noda 2012). However, there was a survey that used interviews to understand alcohol dependence before and after disasters, which found that most post-disaster alcohol dependence was a continuation and relapse from before the disaster, with a new onset rate of 2% (North et al. 2011). Findings from a study after the Great Hanshin-Awaji Earthquake suggest that alcohol consumption does not necessarily increase after the disaster, but that the amount of alcohol consumed may increase among disaster victims who have some health problems (Shimizu et al. (2000), Takatorige 2001).

A survey conducted after the Great Hanshin-Awaji Earthquake revealed that a higher percentage of AA meeting members in the hard-hit areas were relapsed drinkers, and half of the relapsed drinkers were concentrated in the 3 months after the earthquake, suggesting that the earthquake was a trigger. (Noda et al. 1999).

After the Great Hanshin-Awaji Earthquake, the problem of lonely deaths in temporary housing was widely covered by the mass media. However, it has been reported that lonely deaths among alcoholics are common regardless of the disaster, and that there is no significant change before and after the earthquake (Ueno et al. 1998). In other words, alcoholism is a disease that inherently carries a high risk of solitary death. The disaster made it "more visible" in temporary housing, and interventions for alcoholism and alcohol-related problems, which until now have received little attention except from a few specialists, are now taking place.

4.4 Data Collected in the Writing of this Document

The following is a description of the data collected in writing this paper.

1. Target area: Iwate, Miyagi, and Fukushima prefectures where the damage from the Great East Japan Earthquake was extensive and severe.
2. Literature collection (Wakabayashi and Ikoma, 2020): We collected bulletins from local support organizations (e.g., Miyagi Disaster Mental Health Care Center Bulletin/Annual Activity Report, Fukushima Disaster Mental Health Care Center Activity Record Journal) and practice reports (e.g., Alcohol Related Problems Social Workers Association Activity Report, quarterly magazine of Ask Human Care, a citizens' group about addiction-related problems, Be! Be! etc.) were collected.
3. Interview survey

- Subject

7 professionals and self-help group members (1 from Iwate, 4 from Miyagi, 2 from Fukushima) involved in supporting mental health issues including alcohol-related problems in the field

- Procedure

Semi-structured interviews were conducted individually with each subject for one to two hours. The interviews were conducted face-to-face, and were conducted at a location in the subject's area of residence or activity, in order to ensure that others would not overhear the content.

- Ethical considerations

The survey was conducted after obtaining consent from the subjects after explaining in writing and orally that the survey was voluntary, that the subjects would be anonymized, that the data would be handled in a way that would not cause any harm to them, and that they could withdraw their consent during the course of the survey. The study was approved by the Ethics Committee for Research Involving Human Subjects of the University of Tokyo University of Communications. (Totsu Rinken No. 201803).

In addition, since the area does not have a large number of professionals with alcohol-related problems or members of self-help groups, the names of the municipalities have been avoided in the sections of this report where the interview results are mentioned in order to avoid identification of individuals, except in some cases.

4.5 Support for Alcohol-Related Problems in the Three Affected Prefectures

The Great East Japan Earthquake caused damage over a wide area, but this chapter will focus on Fukushima, Miyagi, and Iwate prefectures, which were particularly hard hit.

In December 2011, the Miyagi Mental Health Care Center was established in Sendai City to "promote comprehensive mental health care measures on a long-term basis, including measures to deal with various mental health problems such as PTSD, depression, alcohol abuse, and suicide among disaster victims, community life support for mentally disabled persons in disaster areas, technical support for related organizations, and human resource development. In December 2012, Regional Disaster Mental Health Care Centers were established in Ishinomaki City and Kesennuma City. In Fukushima and Iwate prefectures, Disaster Mental Health Care Centers were established in February 2012.

In June 2012, psychiatrists in Sendai and Ishinomaki City established the Disaster Psychiatric Care Network Miyagi to conduct outreach activities from an office called "Karakoro Station" in Ishinomaki City, and a private psychiatric hospital conducted emergency outreach immediately after the disaster to provide protection to the hospital. In addition, a private psychiatric hospital conducted emergency outreach immediately after the disaster to provide hospital care, and local supporters worked frantically in the midst of severe local psychiatric care suffering from a lack of social resources.

Alcoholism is being treated under the cooperation of the above-mentioned mental health care centers, specialized institutions and organizations, and self-help groups for alcoholics.

4.5.1 There Are Few Medical Institutions with Specialized Beds in the Tohoku Region

Be!(a magazine dealing with addiction in general, difficulties in living growing up in a dysfunctional family, and life skills such as communication and stress coping, based on the National Citizens' Association on Alcohol and Drug Problems, a non-profit corporation), published in March 2012, in November 2011 According to the data presented at the "Tohoku Alcohol-Related Problems Study Group" held in

November 2011 at Tohoku Kai Tohoku Kai Hospital (hereafter referred to as "Tohoku Kai Hospital"), while the percentage of alcoholics among new patients was 34% in the year before the earthquake, it was 45% in May 2011, the second month after the earthquake, and even after that, the percentage remained at 40% until November 2011 at the time of presentation.(The percentage remained in the 40% range until November 2011, when the data was released.

At the time of the earthquake, the Tohoku region was in a situation where the Tohoku Kai Hospital[5] was the only hospital with specialized beds.[6] It is not that there are no other psychiatric hospitals that accept alcoholics, and there are clinics that specialize in outpatient treatment of alcoholics. However, alcoholism should be treated at any psychiatric hospital, but alcohol-related problems tend to be shunned by medical institutions (see below), and the current situation in Japan is that alcoholism is often left to specialized hospitals. Under these circumstances, there are very few hospitals with specialized beds in the 66,889km^2 in the six prefectures of the Tohoku region.

4.5.2 Increase in Alcohol-Related Problems in the Affected Areas

The per capita consumption of alcoholic beverages by prefecture, published by the National Tax Agency, was lower than the national average for all three prefectures in FY2010, but has been increasing since FY2011. 16ℓ (79.2ℓ ⇒ 81.7ℓ). The national average for the same period remained almost the same (81.8ℓ ⇒ 81.6ℓ) (National Tax Agency, 2017).

According to World Medical Association, a certified NPO that has been providing support to the affected areas since April 2011, mainly in Otsuchi Town, Iwate Prefecture, it was around 1 year after the disaster that they noticed a clear increase in the number of consultations related to alcoholism.

The Karakoro Station in Ishinomaki City, Miyagi Prefecture, reported 106 cases in which the main complaint was "alcohol problems" as of 2013, according to the Alcohol-Related Problems Conference (Ota, 2014). According to the newsletter published by the Miyagi Kokoro no Care Center, alcohol-related problems, which were not listed as the main complaint in the "Activity Report from April to July 2012" in Issue 2, were listed in the "Activity Report from August to December

[5]Although it is difficult to define a specialized hospital, it is certain that Tohoku Kai Hospital is involved in the treatment of alcohol dependence, and has opened a specialized ward for alcohol dependence since 1978 (1978); as of 2019, Seinan Hospital in Aomori Prefecture has a specialized alcohol treatment program and is As of 2019, Seinan Hospital in Aomori Prefecture offers a specialized alcohol treatment program and is registered as a specialized medical institution as a consultation base institution in the Comprehensive Support for Addiction Measures Project.

[6]The Japanese Medical Service Law defines hospitals as medical institutions with 20 or more beds and clinics as those with less than 20 beds.

2012" in Issue 3. This indicates that consultations for alcohol-related problems began to be received in the latter half of 2012. Furthermore, according to the "Miyagi Disaster Mental Health Care Center Bulletin No. 4," the number of "addiction problems" in the background breakdown of consultations received by the Miyagi Disaster Mental Health Care Center (total number of cases, multiple choice) was 1062 in 2013 (2013), 1549 in 2014 (2014), 1454 in 2015 (2015) In 2012, the number was 1454, accounting for a high percentage of consultations (see Fig. 4.1).

Addiction" means "addiction" and broadly refers to dependence. The Miyagi Disaster Mental Health Care Center Bulletin, from which this article is taken, explains addiction as follows: "Addiction is a predilection for a particular substance, behavior, or relationship. It is the tendency to prefer certain substances, behaviors, or relationships in particular. It refers to indulging in bad habits that one cannot stop

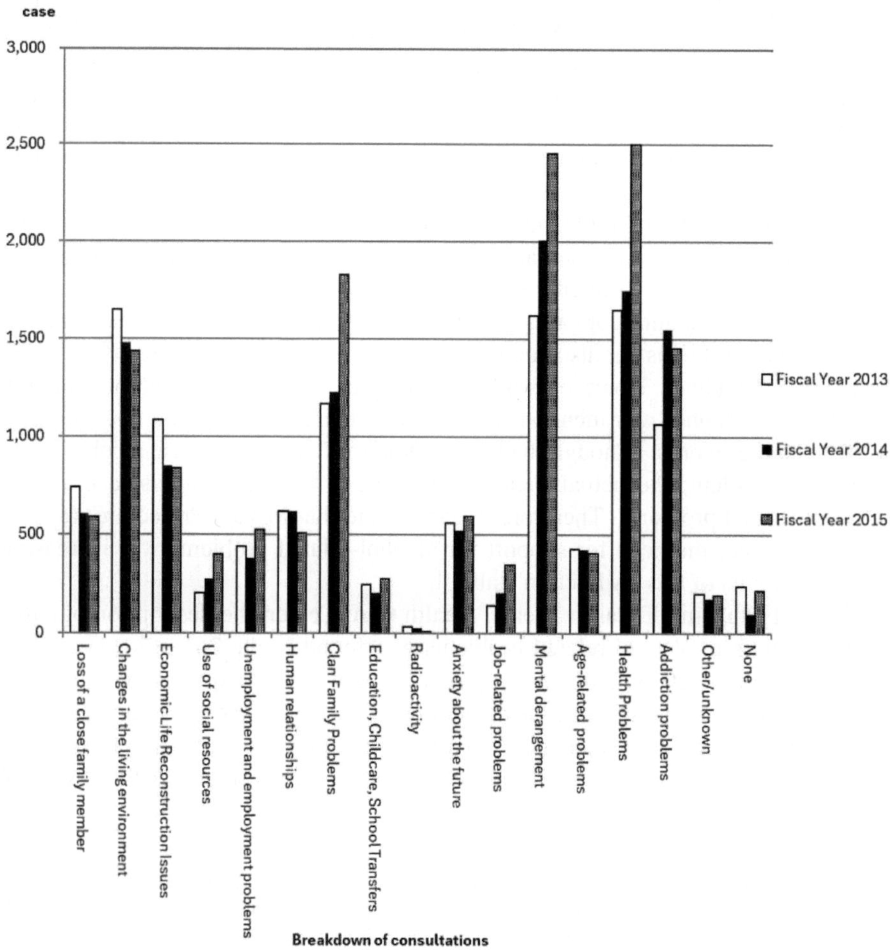

Fig. 4.1 Breakdown of consultations at the Miyagi Disaster Mental Health Care Center. Source: Miyagi Disaster Mental Health Care Center (2016)

Table 4.1 Details of guidance and advice from professional positions

Guidance and advice from a specialist's perspective Details	Cases
Alcohol-related problems	107
Problems with gambling	5
Drug problems	4
Depression	24
Complicated grief	6
PTSD	10
Abuse	56
Others	232

Source: Miyagi Disaster Mental Health Care Center (2016)

even though one wants to. In Miyagi Prefecture, there is a specialized treatment facility for addiction, Tohoku Kai Hospital, which accepts patients with addictions not only to alcohol, but also to drugs, gambling, and shopping. However, diagnostic criteria for behavioral addictions such as gambling and shopping addictions have not yet stabilized,[7] and the term "addiction" is thought to be the most inclusive of all the terms used to describe addiction, and the study group focusing on addiction that is actually held in Miyagi Prefecture, mainly at the Tohoku-kai Hospital, is called the "Miyagi Addiction Study Group". In other words, it is assumed that the number of cases of addiction other than alcoholism is also included in this tally. When we look at the total of "details of guidance and advice from a professional standpoint"(total number of cases, multiple choice) (see Table 4.1), we see that not only alcohol problems but also gambling and drug problems were mentioned in the content of the advice. However, while gambling and drugs were mentioned in only a few cases, alcohol was mentioned in an overwhelmingly large number of cases (107). In other words, although the label "addiction" is used because alcohol is not the only problem, the actual breakdown suggests that it is almost exclusively alcohol-related problems. Therefore, it can be said that Miyagi Prefecture was in a situation where the need for support for alcohol-related problems was increasing with the results of this "Addiction" tally.

In the Fukushima Disaster Mental Health Care Center, the description of cases and responses to alcohol-related problems was found in the 2012 (2012) activity report, and in the 2013 (2013) activity report, the word "alcohol" is mentioned 44 times, and the number of sentences touching on the importance of intervention for alcohol-related problems increased from the previous year. According to an interview with the editors of the quarterly Be! 's Editorial Department (2014), "Alcohol

[7] For example, Internet dependence is not classified in the International Statistical Classification of Diseases and Related Health Problems tenth edition (ICD-10) established by the World Health Organization (WHO). Related Health Problems tenth edition (ICD-10), which was formulated by the World Health Organization (WHO), but was included in ICD-11.

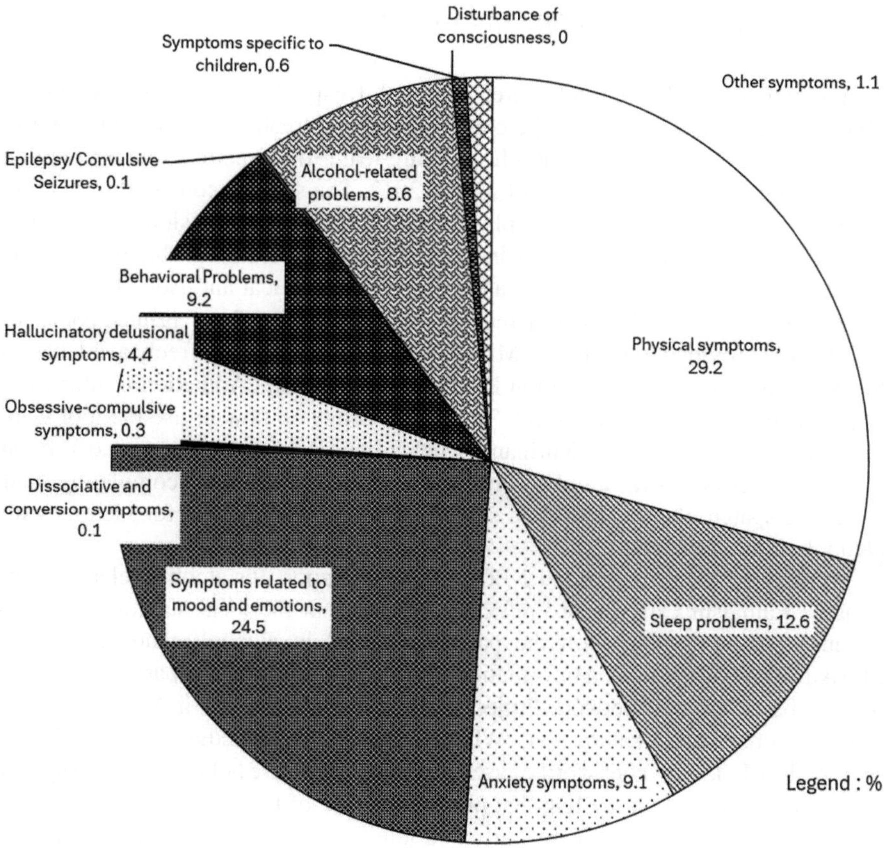

Fig. 4.2 Breakdown of "Symptomatic" in the background of consultation at Fukushima Disaster Mental Health Care Center. Source: Fukushima Disaster Mental Health Care Center (2015a, 2015b)

accounts for a significant percentage of the problems that come up from the temporary housing.

From January to February 2014, Fukushima Prefecture conducted an "Evacuee Opinion Survey" of over 60,000 evacuees in and out of the prefecture. 67.5% of the households had someone complaining of physical or mental illness, and of those, 22.6% said that their drinking and smoking had increased.

According to Fukushima Disaster Mental Health Care Center (2015a, 2015b), 74.2% of the 4973 total consultation support persons had some symptoms, of which 525 were "drinking problems" (the population number is 6112 due to multiple selection) (see Fig. 4.2).

4.5.3 Support from Across the Country

At the request of Iwate Prefecture, National Hospital Organization Kurihama Medical and Addiction Center, the oldest specialized treatment center for alcoholism in Japan, dispatched a mental health care team to Ofunato, Iwate Prefecture, from March 24, 2011, to the end of March 2012. The support consisted of visiting disaster victims and examining people with grief reactions, depression, and alcohol-related problems. Anticipating an increase in alcohol-related problems after the disaster, National Hospital Organization Kurihama Medical and Addiction Center developed a "Drinking Problem Screening and Intervention Tool," printed copies of which were provided to Iwate and Miyagi prefectures, and made freely available on the National Hospital Organization Kurihama Medical and Addiction Center website (where it is still posted today). Training sessions on how to use the tool were held for local support staff (Kurihama Medical and Addiction Center, n.d.). In an article in the Kanagawa Shimbun on April 6, 2012, shortly after completing their term of dispatch, the support team stressed the need for support for victims with alcohol-related problems.

Morikawa (2013), a certified NPO, provided support for alcohol-related problems in Kamaishi City, Iwate Prefecture. Seeing that the local support staff was exhausted from dealing with the parties involved in alcohol-related problems, Morikawa (2012) created an information sharing system with each party in the community, based on the "Network Project for Alcohol and Health" in Yokkaichi City, Mie Prefecture, and centered on "What is Safety," "Knowledge for Safety," and "Strengths Model, In other words, case study meetings were held to provide support for supporters based on the line that protects the life of the party, the safety of the surroundings, the security of the party and family, and the strength (goodness and power) of the party.

As a supplement to the current situation in Iwate Prefecture, where these supports were provided, the Iwate Disaster Mental Health Care Center is operated by Iwate Medical University on consignment, in cooperation with the Mental Health Welfare Center, public health centers, and other administrative agencies. In addition, the Iwate Mental Health Welfare Center holds alcohol and drug addiction case study meetings on a regular basis.

In Miyagi Prefecture, in August 2011, Ishinomaki City requested Tohoku-kai Hospital to provide support for drinking problems in temporary housing, but Tohoku-kai Hospital alone did not have the manpower to do so.,[8] and the Japan Association of Social Workers on Alcohol-Related Problems (hereinafter referred to as the ASW Association) dispatched personnel. (The ASW Association's support was later extended not only to Ishinomaki City, but also to Onagawa City and Higashimatsushima City.) The social workers dispatched by the ASW Association,

---

[8] Immediately after the earthquake, Tohoku Kai Hospital had staff go to each affected area in Miyagi Prefecture, not limited to Sendai, upon request, to provide support to aid workers and visit various locations (Japan Alcohol Social Workers Association (2015)).

who were experienced in alcohol problems, intervened together with support staff such as public health nurses who had no experience in intervening in addiction, so that local staff could recognize alcohol problems and intervene at an early stage. The local staff is now able to recognize and intervene in alcohol-related problems at an early stage (Fujita, 2015).

In establishing the extensive support system described below in Fukushima Prefecture, Hizen Psychiatric Center and other specialized organizations across Japan provided training and other support.

4.5.4 Support Centered on Specialized Support Organizations

In Miyagi Prefecture, the specialty hospitals that originally formed the core of support in Miyagi Prefecture have formed relationships with local communities and self-help groups on a daily basis, and a dependency support network has been established (Izumi and Wakabayashi 2013), which some support staff said led to easier collaboration after the earthquake (Editorial Department of the quarterly Be! 2012a, 2012b). Based on these relationships, various support organizations continued to engage in long-lasting support activities and seemed to be nurturing their supporters as they worked while emphasizing support for supporters. The author once attended a case study meeting held in Miyagi Prefecture, and it was apparent that the supporters were carefully involved with the parties concerned and were able to form trusting relationships with them.

The Miyagi Alcoholics Anonymous operates "Campus Donguri," a welfare facility for alcoholics, and after the disaster, the association was able to smoothly communicate with the government and medical services, and did not have to fight alone, which we believe is a result of the network building.

In the Miyagi Disaster Mental Health Care Center (2016), Tohoku Kai Hospital, Miyagi Prefecture Alcoholics Anonymous (a non-profit organization affiliated with the All Japan Alcoholics Anonymous Federation, a public interest incorporated association in Miyagi Prefecture. Hereinafter referred to as "Miyagi Alcoholics Anonymous") and ASW Association as cooperating organizations for alcohol-related issues. The Tohoku Kai Hospital and the ASW Association are involved in support and network coordination activities, while the Miyagi Alcoholics Anonymous is commissioned by the Miyagi Disaster Mental Health Care Center to conduct various types of meetings in Kesennuma, Ishinomaki, Higashimatsushima, and Natori. The Miyagi Prefecture Alcoholics Anonymous seminar held on February 11, 2020, mentioned that the Motoyoshi, Natori, and Shichigahama branches of the Miyagi Prefecture Alcoholics Anonymous Association were established after the earthquake, and that they have left their mark in increasing the number of social resources such as self-help groups in the community.

As an organization specializing in outreach, Karakoro Station has provided support for victims suffering from alcohol-related problems through a wide range of activities, such as medical consultation recommendations during visits, environmental adjustments, lectures, events, and meetings in cooperation with local AAs.

In Ishinomaki City, Miyagi Prefecture, a very interesting practice was found to be taking place. For example, the Karakoro Station held "Ojikoro," where men gathered in the morning to cook together and in the afternoon participated in their favorite recreational activities, such as Shogi and karaoke. In the afternoon, they would participate in their favorite recreational activities, such as Shogi and karaoke. The Miyagi Kokoro Care Center Ishinomaki Regional Center conducted the "Kokoko Farm Project" and provided a place to change one's mood and socialize through the cultivation of vegetables and flowers. This was against the backdrop that men find it difficult to gather at salons and drink because they have nothing to do. Considering that men have a higher rate of suicide attempts than women (Japan Suicide Countermeasures Promotion Center, n.d.), it can be said that the practice in Ishinomaki has left a significant achievement in community mental health welfare.

Even when interventions can be made for alcohol-related problems, the process to sobriety and the difficulty of maintaining sobriety can be painful and time-consuming, making it difficult to achieve results, such as the death of a party. In addition, drunken parties may intimidate supporters, and support is needed to prevent supporters from holding on to hurtful experiences (Editorial Board of the quarterly Be! magazine 2012). The issue of supporter support has been discussed in the previous chapter, and it will continue to be important to ensure that supporters have a place to share their pain with each other, such as through self-help groups, study groups, and case study meetings, and to have a network of supporters who can support each other at any time. Miyagi Prefecture has the potential to provide a model of a support network, where supporters have a place to share with each other under the supervision of a specialized treatment facility.

4.5.5 Massive Reinforcement of Support System

In Fukushima Prefecture, there are no specialized hospitals with beds, and there is only one institution (Oshima Clinic) that has long been involved in alcohol treatment. However, the history of AA meetings is older than that of other prefectures in the Tohoku region, and the number of members is larger than the population of other prefectures in the Tohoku region. In 2013, the activities of self-help groups in Fukushima resumed when the AA meetings in Minamisoma were restored. However, due to a lack of venues for the meetings described below, the number of meetings has decreased from before the disaster.

In light of the above situation, in April 2014, the Fukushima Disaster Mental Health Care Center organized the "Alcohol Project" to implement the Community Alcohol Response Enhancement Project. It holds workshops, lectures, symposiums, and public lectures for citizens, and the symposiums are attended by members of self-help groups by alcoholics in Fukushima Prefecture. In addition, the Center developed model projects in selected areas. In Iwaki, training sessions for supporters and alcohol education for residents; in Soso, educational activities at high schools, fire stations, temporary housing, etc.; study sessions and case study meetings in collaboration with Hibarigaoka Hospital; training at Karakoro Station; and preparations for starting an AA meeting in Soma City were conducted. In 2015, the word "alcohol" appeared 189 times in the "Alcoholism Report" and lectures for residents and alcohol-related family classes were held in various locations, and the response to alcohol-related problems is being strengthened. In particular, in the Soso District, where the model project is being implemented, the AA meetings that had been under preparation since fiscal year 2014 have finally been launched, and the development of social resources has been a success. The staff of the Fukushima Disaster Mental Health Care Center always attends the training sessions of the Tohoku Branch of the ASW Association, to which the author belongs, and their enthusiasm for building a support network for alcohol-related problems is evident. The "Men's Gathering" has been held in Fukushima as a male-focused approach. They also held a joint event with "Ojikoro" in Miyagi Prefecture as described in the previous section (Fukushima Disaster Mental Health Care Center 2015a, 2015b).

The reason for this is that Fukushima Prefecture, where there were many suicides related to the Great East Japan Earthquake, became aware of the crisis. In providing support, they were aware of the public health perspective, and were conscious of a simple intervention that included sobriety, regardless of whether or not there was a diagnosis of addiction.

Although the background is that alcohol-related problems have become more serious in the wake of the catastrophe and have had to be confronted, the Fukushima Prefecture "Alcohol Project" is an example of a large-scale effort to build a support network for alcohol-related problems in the region, and it is a commendable initiative.

4.5.6 Efforts to Prevent Isolation

The aforementioned Fukushima Prefecture alcohol project is not only a large-scale public health measure, but also a steady support project. For example, as part of the project, the Soma Regional Center for Mental Health Care, Nagomi, is focusing its efforts on addressing the problem of alcohol consumption among elderly men living alone. The "Men's Gathering" meetings are held to provide a place for middle-aged and older men who tend to isolate themselves, and users who have increased their drinking due to loneliness have been able to continue their sobriety after participating in these meetings (Tsukamoto 2020).

As a countermeasure against isolation, "Ojikoro" at the Karakoro Station in Ishinomaki City, Miyagi Prefecture, is a program to prevent male isolation, and the

Miyagi Disaster Mental Health Care Center also attempted to "gather" to prevent isolation in a way not limited to alcohol-related problems. For example, they provided a place where only evacuees from the nuclear power plant evacuation area could gather, and provided a place where they could be involved in a safe situation without the risk of being hurt by comments from those around them who did not understand them.

There are also efforts to establish new group centers in areas where there are few self-help groups, and the number of self-help group centers is increasing in Fukushima and Miyagi prefectures.

4.6 After the Support[9]

4.6.1 Geographical Factors

However, in some areas, the problem of depopulation and the shortage of supporters themselves has risen, while in others, the aging of the population has made it difficult to increase the local response capacity.

The difficulties in mobility are not limited to the elderly, but also include those who are in the prime of their working lives, and the area of the health center is not so large in terms of population, but is vast in terms of area.

However, in some areas in the Tohoku region, the Internet environment is still not in place, and in areas where there are many elderly people, there are many people who have difficulty using the Internet as a tool. Although there is no lack of people who can provide support, we have heard from several subjects that the areas where support is needed are too large to accommodate their needs.

Another issue is that the aging of the population makes it difficult for people to move around, which is necessary to form a support network. In the Tohoku region, each municipality covers a large area, and it is often difficult to move people from one region to another, making cooperation difficult. While some self-help groups received support from neighboring areas, such as participation in meetings, there were also areas where information sharing within self-help groups was not possible due to the difficulty of moving within the prefecture itself. It is difficult for the elderly to move around in an area that is large and depopulated, and where public transportation is unlikely to be developed. In areas where there is a shortage of human resources who can provide support, the promotion of remote support is urgently needed.

---

[9] The data used in this paper is from Wakabayashi (2024), and some of the content and results are also duplicated.

4.6.2 Changes in Residents' Awareness After the Earthquake

As for changes after the earthquake, the respondents felt that the local residents' desire for assistance had increased and that they felt a change in awareness of alcohol-related problems in the community as a whole.

Some of the respondents also indicated that they have sensed a change in the awareness of alcohol-related problems among their supporters.

Since addiction is associated with low help-seeking ability, we believe that "the culture of 'consulting with others when in trouble' had not taken root, and the awareness that 'it is OK to consult with someone' has emerged," is a significant change from the perspective of primary prevention.

If, in addition to this, the awareness of the community has also changed, this would suggest that the groundwork for early intervention in alcohol-related problems has been laid.

4.6.3 Impact of Change in Support Personnel

It has been pointed out that there is an issue of retention because of the frequent transfer of staff when the activities are administratively driven (Kanno, Maeda, Ogata, et al., 2022). On the other hand, some regions have begun to take action to address this issue, and some participants who have been transferred to a new department have been given the opportunity to gather again in the form of step-up training, and interviews have been conducted to find out the status of the department where the person in charge of the training was located.

The common denominator in all regions is that it will take time to raise the level of support for any one issue in the entire region, as each municipality has a variety of support issues. This needs to be addressed from the perspective of how to build a regional network. For this purpose, one of the results of this survey was to try to reconnect people who have once gained a deeper understanding of alcohol-related issues through training, which may be effective in terms of increasing the "fulcrums of the network.

4.6.4 Impact of the "Corona Disaster"

Several respondents reported that the so-called "Corona disaster" prevented them from conducting "gathering" activities such as group work, group psychotherapy, and self-help groups, which play an important role in supporting addicts. The aforementioned efforts to prevent isolation were blocked. Although some efforts were made to reduce the number of participants and to use screens, it is undeniable that this was a major disincentive to gathering together. For example, at the Soma Regional Mental Health Care Center, Nagomi, the number of consultations increased, partly due to the increased recognition of the center as a consultation center, but also due to the fact that there were several cases of alcohol abuse due to reduced contact with others after the Corona disaster (Tsukamoto 2021).

Another impact was the proliferation of online training. Online training, which used to be difficult to attend from rural areas due to time and financial constraints, is now available online, which has lowered the hurdle to attending training in early intervention programs for alcohol-related problems. However, while the online availability has made it easier to participate in the training, it has also made it harder to form the relationships that form the foundation of the network, such as becoming friends through the training.

In addition, some respondents reported an increase in hospitalizations of their self-help group members after the earthquake, possibly due to stress. Although it is difficult to make a definite statement because the group is already aging, the respondents feel that the number of hospitalizations and collapses of members has increased after the Great East Japan Earthquake.

The spread of the use of online training throughout the world is one of the positive effects of the "Corona Disaster," and it is expected that online training will expand the base for the acquisition of knowledge and skills through training. From the viewpoint of building relationships and networks, it is necessary to devise ways to build relationships, such as by holding online seminars.

The impact of the "corona disaster" is still far from being eliminated even now that COVID-19 has become a category 5 infectious disease, so it is necessary to continue to investigate the impact of the disease.

4.6.5 Others

Some said that it has become difficult to uncover drinking problems because the victims have moved from temporary housing to public housing (Be!'s Editorial Department, 2018), some communities have suffered from the loss of rent subsidies after 12 years have passed, and that the increase in paperwork in the entire interpersonal field has made it difficult to "lean in" to the victims. Some people said that they could no longer spend time on "staying close" due to the increase in paperwork in the entire interpersonal field.

It is difficult to actively participate in self-help group activities if a person is old and has a serious illness. This may have influenced the decrease in the number of so-called "active members" of self-help groups.

4.7 Recommendations on Support for Alcohol-Related Problems

The author believes that the problem of supporting supporters, which was mentioned in the previous chapter, may have been more pronounced in the alcohol-related problems. This is because there are very few supporters who specialize in alcohol-related problems, not only alcohol-related problems, but also addiction and addiction-related problems. Under such circumstances, the number of consultations on alcohol-related problems in the affected areas is large, and many of the supporters there are unable to respond. Nevertheless, the number of supporters with specialized knowledge and skills is far too small to keep up. It was imperative to create a system that would enable local supporters to deal with alcohol-related problems on their own. Domestic and international experts were well aware of this situation and consistently focused their activities on supporting supporters.

Due to its intractability and the difficulty of initial intervention, alcoholism has a history of being marginalized by psychiatry and becoming a specialized medical condition. Emphasizing the need for specialty care encourages the tendency to leave it to specialty care (Noda 2012). Based on this experience, we strongly hope that supporters in other communities will take an interest in alcohol-related problems on a regular basis and form a support network so that they can always be ready to respond in cooperation with various organizations. In fact, the number of people suffering from alcohol-related problems is not large enough to be covered by existing specialized medical institutions.

Recommendations are made in light of this situation.

4.7.1 Raise the Level of Response to Alcohol-Related Problems

The first step in providing support for alcohol-related problems in the affected areas is for those who are involved with the victims to become aware of the alcohol-related problems in the background of the victims' lives. While accepting the pain of the victims, it is desirable to support them in the long term to achieve sobriety in the case of pre-alcoholics and abstinence from alcohol in the case of alcohol-dependent patients, It is desirable to support the survivor to become aware of alcohol-related problems in the background of his/her life.

However, these are exactly the same demands made of Japan's mental health and welfare field with regard to alcohol-related problems, and not just in disaster-stricken areas.

We have the impression that in the affected areas, the earthquake has triggered a growing interest in alcohol-related issues and a widening circle of initiatives. According to the stories of supporters in various areas, while there are cases where problem drinking has progressed after the earthquake, as was the case in the Great Hanshin-Awaji Earthquake, there are also many cases where the Great East Japan

Earthquake led to the discovery of alcohol problems that had been hidden from the outside world (relatives other than family members living together, children living far away, etc.), which led to intervention. This may be a small "blessing in disguise" in the wake of the horrific damage caused by the earthquake.

Because alcohol-related problems tend to be hidden by the person concerned and those around them for fear of prejudice, it is important to increase the sensitivity of supporters to alcohol-related problems and to intervene by recognizing problems even from the slightest sign.

As a further tailwind, The Basic Act on Measures against Alcohol-rerated Health Harm (hereinafter referred to as the "Basic Act") was enacted in 2013, and the implementation of the Basic Plan for the Promotion of Measures against Alcohol and Health Disorders (hereinafter referred to as the "Basic Plan") has begun in various places. The Basic Act is a philosophy law, and its basic principles are to "implement appropriate preventive measures in accordance with each stage of the development, progression, and relapse of alcohol health disorders, and to support people to lead smooth daily and social lives," and to "give necessary consideration to ensure organic coordination with measures for problems such as drunken driving, violence, abuse, and suicide. and "necessary consideration to ensure organic coordination with policies on problems such as drunk driving, violence, abuse, and suicide" (Article 3).

The Basic Act also imposes obligations on the national government, local governments, businesses, citizens, doctors, and health promotion business operators. The national and local governments are to formulate and implement measures and policies (Articles 4 and 5), businesses (meaning businesses that manufacture or sell alcoholic beverages) are to cooperate with these measures and take care to prevent the occurrence, progress, and recurrence of alcohol-related health problems (Article 6), and the public is to be aware of alcohol-related problems (alcohol-related health problems and related problems such as drunk driving, violence, abuse, and suicide). (Article 6), and that the public shall cooperate with these measures and give consideration to the prevention of the occurrence, progression and recurrence of alcohol-related health problems (alcohol-related health problems and related problems such as drunk driving, violence, abuse and suicide. The same shall apply hereinafter). (Article 7), and that physicians and other medical personnel and health promotion service providers shall cooperate with the measures for alcohol-related health problems implemented by the national and local governments (Articles 8 and 9). (Article 8), and doctors and other medical personnel shall endeavor to provide quality and appropriate medical care for alcohol-related health problems (Article 8). Article 22 also specifies support for alcoholics' organizations and self-help groups, the importance of which was mentioned in the first half of this chapter.

And one of the major characteristics of this Basic Act is the large number of related ministries and agencies. Article 25 states that "The government shall establish a Council for the Promotion of Measures to Cope with Alcohol Health Disorders, which shall consist of officials from the Cabinet Office, Ministry of Justice, Ministry of Finance, Ministry of Education, Culture, Sports, Science and Technology, Ministry of Health, Labor and Welfare, National Police Agency, and other relevant administrative agencies. This is in response to the wide range of impact alcohol-related problems have. (Wakabayashi 2016).

The movement of this Basic Act and Basic Plan should change the awareness of alcohol-related problems in Japan as a whole, and increase the country's overall ability to deal with alcohol-related problems in the wake of disasters. There are not a few opportunities to provide information. For example, the ASW Association is holding a basic alcoholism recovery support course for social workers in response to the implementation of the Basic Act, and the All Japan Federation of Alcoholics Anonymous is also holding seminars for the public. The All Japan Federation of Alcoholics Anonymous also holds seminars for the general public. During "Alcohol-Related Problem Awareness Week," as specified in the Basic Act, awareness-raising activities are held throughout Japan, and the Ministry of Health, Labor and Welfare has created a page on its website to provide information on measures against addiction.

Each of the three prefectures has clearly stated measures to deal with alcohol-related problems among disaster victims. Iwate Prefecture has a section entitled "Consideration for the victims of the Great East Japan Earthquake and Tsunami" in "III Basic Concept of the Plan 3 Perspectives of Efforts," which clearly states that measures for alcohol-related health problems will be taken in conjunction with mental health care measures in the event of a disaster.

Fukushima Prefecture established a section entitled "Support for Alcohol-Related Issues in Consideration of the Impact of the Great East Japan Earthquake," which included five descriptions of the current situation and efforts.

Miyagi Prefecture presents the common content of its efforts regardless of whether there was a disaster or not, but provides data on the number of alcohol-related problems caused by the Great East Japan Earthquake as background for the increase in alcohol-related problems, and includes careful descriptions of the support provided at the time of the Great East Japan Earthquake.

All three prefectures will continue their support activities for alcohol-related problems in the affected areas, mainly by providing support for self-help groups in the affected areas and various training and awareness programs.

4.7.2 Difficulties in "Intervention for Alcohol Consumption" in the Affected Areas and the Burnout of Supporters

Next, I will discuss the difficulty of "intervention for alcohol consumption" in supporting disaster victims. In recent years, intervention for alcoholism has shifted from the old "bottoming out model (waiting until the person realizes that he/she cannot handle it on their own)" to "brief intervention (early intervention)" and "intervention on the amount of alcohol consumption including sobriety," but both involve the same intervention on alcohol consumption. However, in a situation where episodes such as, "When I asked a person to cut back on alcohol, I was told,

'Then give me back my family,'" or "I couldn't say 'stop drinking' to a victim who lost his family in the earthquake and told me his horrific experience," are common, the kind of intervention that is usually used to treat alcoholics is not likely to work. In such a situation, the kind of efforts that are usually made to treat alcoholics often do not work. Based on the experience of support activities after the Great Hanshin-Awaji Earthquake, some people have said that offering to abstain from alcohol makes it difficult to build a relationship and does not lead to positive results (Noda 2012). Rather than intervening in drinking problems, it is necessary to first get close to the victims' feelings and build a relationship of trust with them.

The attitude of being attentive to the thoughts of the subject in front of you is rather foundational to the concept of support in the social welfare field. However, even supporters who have been involved in alcohol-related problems for many years are not necessarily accustomed to careful involvement in the background of drinking problems, unless they are accustomed to outreach, because they are targeting a population with some willingness to be treated. Thus, the difficulty of intervening in drinking indicates that support for alcohol-related problems in the affected areas may be challenging even for those that have been involved in alcoholism support. Those who have experience with alcohol-related problems can still consider the particularities of working with disaster victims based on their past experience, but it is not difficult to imagine that those who do not have a foundation in this area will find it extremely difficult to intervene in alcohol-related problems in the disaster area. Again, alcohol-related problems have been marginalized in the mental health and welfare field, and few people have experience in providing support. For this reason, support for supporters in the affected areas by specialists is necessary. It is important for supporters in the affected areas to share their difficulties with others while receiving supervision from experts to prevent burnout among supporters.

4.7.3 Based on the Interview 12 Years Later

Many of the supporters targeted in this study indicated that as a result of the various efforts, they felt a positive sense of change in the community's awareness of and response to alcohol-related problems. They also described positive changes, albeit in clinical terms, in what was documented. This may indicate that the community can change if support is provided.

Nevertheless, it has been 12 years since the Great East Japan Earthquake occurred, and while other major disasters have occurred in the meantime, one of the reasons why we dare to focus on the Great East Japan Earthquake is because of geographical and regional factors. We believe that the Great East Japan Earthquake brought into sharp relief the problems of the Tohoku region, which is vastly damaged, depopulated, and aging. The aging of the population is progressing faster than the aid that has been provided, and the difficulty of building a network due to geographical problems is still an issue 12 years later.

As one of the countermeasures, we believe that it is urgent to establish a "remote connection" environment represented by the Internet for all people, regardless of whether they are supporters or parties involved. Although some data pointed out the limitations of the Internet connection, it is useful from the viewpoints of triggers for connection and acquisition of knowledge, and its introduction is urgently needed in order to support a vast area with limited human resources.

On the other hand, if there is even one person at the entrance who can "lean in" and teach the current Internet conferencing system, there may be a circle that expands from there. I am concerned that this may not be the case. The results of this study clearly indicate the need for "support to lean on" and "connections with others," but in this vast disaster area and in the vast aged and depopulated region, we may have reached the stage where "physical environment for connections" is necessary.

4.8 Conclusion

Finally, in considering alcohol-related problems in the emergency situation of a disaster, I would like to share with you about "normalcy that becomes abnormal. Supporters who were involved in providing support for alcohol-related problems in the disaster areas are keenly aware of the importance of "health to be abnormal" in a situation that is not normal, and that a campaign such as "Let's all get sick in peace" is needed (Suzuki 2012). The author strongly sympathizes with this idea. It would be unnatural for no one to get sick during a disaster emergency, and if alcohol-related problems arise as one of the reactions, it would be a natural one. The important thing is not to "not get sick," but to share and support each other's recovery when we do get sick.

And as mentioned earlier, after the Corona disaster, that sharing and support has reached a turning point.

References

Be!'s Editorial Department (2012a) "Working to Tackle Alcohol-Related Problems in Temporary Housing," *Be!*, 106, 26–29.

Be!'s Editorial Department (2012b) "From the Disaster Area—How Do You Intervene with Someone Who Says, "Even if I Die from Drinking, it's Worth it"?", *Be!*, 109, 22–25.

Be!'s Editorial Department (2014) "The Impact of the Nuclear Accident on the Human Psyche: Working to Address the Drinking Problem in Fukushima," *Be!*, 116, 22–26.

Be!'s Editorial Department (2018) "Uncovering! Addiction Collaboration Model 2 Miyagi," *Be!*, 133, 82–87.

Fujita, S. (2015) "Project to Support Victims of the Great East Japan Earthquake: Report on Support Activities by the Japan Social Worker Association for Alcohol Related Problems in Ishinomaki," Japan Social Worker Association for Alcohol Related Problems ed., *30th*

Anniversary Commemorative Magazine of Japan Social Worker Association for Alcohol Related problems, 23–27.

Fukushima Disaster Mental Health Care Center (2015a) *Fukushima Disaster Mental Health Care Center Activity Record Magazine.*

Fukushima Disaster Mental Health Care Center (2015b) *Fukushima Disaster Mental Health Care Center Activity Report of "Alcohol Project".*

Higuchi, S. (2007) "Current Status and Future Prospects of Alcoholism Treatment," *Psychiatria et Neurologia Japonica*, 109(6), 534–535.

Ino, A., T. Okoshi and Y. Okumiya (1991) "Short-term and Long-term Prognosis of Alcoholism—From a Follow-up Survey of Danshukai Members—," *Psychiatria et Neurologia Japonica,* 93(5), 334–358.

Iwata, Y. (2010) *Self-help Movements and New Social Work Practices,* Tyuohoki-Syuppan, pp.53–54.

Izumi, H. and M. Wakabayashi (2013) "The Recovery Support Network for Addiction in Sendai: on the Cooperative Relationships between 'T' Hospital and Selp-help Goups," *Tohoku Bunka Kenkyujo Kiyo*, 56, 21–37.

Kanno T., M. Maeda, J. Ogata, S. Ishikawa, I. Watabe et al. (2022) "Symposium 2 Victims of Disasters and Alcohol Problems: Consider Reconstruction from Disaster and Care and Support during the COVID-19 Pandemic "Alcohol Project" in Fukushima Disaster Mental Health Care Center: Family Class Initiatives," *Japanese Alcohol, Nicotine & Drug Addiction Conference 2022 Program and Abstract Collection,* p.178.

Kubo, A. (2004) *Self-help Groups —Focusing on Those Affected—*, Aikawa-Syobo, p.14.

Japan Suicide Countermeasures Promotion Center. http://jssc.ncnp.go.jp/archive/old_csp/oldupdate.html

Kimura, H. (2014) "Listen, Learn and Think about the Great East Japan Earthquake," Miyagi Association of Psychiatric Social Workers, *I want to convey it, I want to connect it. 3.11—Great East Japan Earthquake and Miyagi PSW: a Collection of Practical Records of Psychiatric Social Workers,* 165–171.

Kurihama Medical and Addiction Center. http://www.kurihama-med.jp/shinsai/

Miyagi Disaster Mental Health Care Center (2016) *Bulletin of the Miyagi Disaster Mental Health Care Center,* 4.

Morikawa, S. (2012) Make a Starting Point of Collaboration for Alcohol-Related Problems. *Be!,*108, 44–47.

Morikawa, S. (2013) "Attempts to Support Alcoholics in Areas Affected by the Great East Japan Earthquake—Support Activities in Kamaishi City, Iwate Prefecture," *Community Health*, 19–25.

National Tax Agency (2017) *Sake Report*, p. 48.

Noda, T. (2012) "Alcohol Related Problems following a Disaster: Intermediate and Long Term Psychiatric Problems of the Great 2011 Tohoku Earthquake," *Clinical Psychiatry*, 54(11), 1079–1086.

Noda, T., T. Aso, S. Shimizu et al. (1999) "The Impact of the Great Hanshin-Awaji Earthquake on Danshukai in the Disaster Area (second report)—The Actual Situation of Alcoholics Danshukai Members after the Earthquake," *Journal of the Japanese Sociery of Social Psychiatry,* 7, 225–238.

Noda, T., A. Kawada, T. Ando, K. Oishi, K. Hirano, H. Imamichi, M. Kurauchi, Y. Iwata and O. Hiyama (1988) "Survey on the Actual Condition of Alcoholics in a Satellite City—Takatsuki City—and a Follow-up Study—in Relation to a Community Support System—," *Japanese Medical Society of Alcohol Studies*, 23(1), 26–52.

Noguchi, Y. (1996) *The Sociology of Alcoholism,* Nihon-Hyoronsya, pp. 30–51.

North, C. S., C. L. Ringwalt, D. Downs et al. (2011) "Postdisaster Course of Alcohol Use Disorders in Systematically Studied Survivors of 10 Disasters," *Arch Gen Psychiatry*, 68, 173–180.

Ota, Y. (2014) "Report on Support Activities for Alcohol-Related Problems in the Affected Areas," *The Journal of the Japanese Society of Alcohol-Related Problems*, 16(1), 186–190.

Okazaki, S. (2014) "Chapter 3 Movements of the Miyagi Association of Psychiatric Social Workers: Activities of the Sendai Disaster Mental Health Care Team "About the Mobile Counseling Service at Evacuation Centers"," Miyagi Association of Psychiatric Social Workers, *I want to convey it, I want to connect it. 3.11—Great East Japan Earthquake and Miyagi PSW: a Collection of Practical Records of Psychiatric Social Workers,* 133–138.

Shimizu, S., T. Aso, T. Noda et al. (2000) "Natural Disasters and Alcohol Consumption in Cultural Context; the Great Hanshin Earthquake in Japan," *Addiction,* 95, 529–536.

Suzuki, T. (2012) "Disaster Relief, Support and Addiction—3.11 at a Psychiatric Hospital," *Journal of Addiction and Family,* 28(4), 251–255.

Senzaki, A. (2016) "Typical Mental Disorders," in Japan Association of Schools for Training Mental Health and Welfare Workers ed. *New Mental Health Worker Training Course, Vol. 1, Mental Disordernd their Treatment* 2nd ed., Chuohoki Publishing, 97–100.

Takatorige, T. (2001) "Drinking Habits and Characteristics of Urban Male Residents with High Alcohol Intake—Analysis of Temporary Housing Residents after the Great Hanshin Earthquake—," *Japanese Journal of Public Health,* 48, 344–355.

Tsukamoto, K. (2020) "Fukushima: What are the Measures against Alcoholic in the Affected Areas?," *Be!*, 138, 50–51.

Tsukamoto, K. (2021) "Ten years after the Great East Japan Earthquake: Psychological Care for the Corona Disaster in Fukushima," *Be!* 142, 46–49.

Ueno, Y., H. Syuta, M. Asano et al. (1998) "Comparison of Mortality Patterns of Persons Living Alone in Kobe before and after the Southern Hyogo Earthquake," *Report of Research Center for Urban Safety and Security,* Kobe University, 2, 279–284.

Yamamoto, Y. (2015) "The Psychology of Addiction," in Yamamoto, Y. ed. *Addiction Approach for Human Services—Understanding the Addicted Mind and Support for Hardness of Life,* Chuohoki Publishing, 31–46.

Wakabayashi, M. (2016) "The Basic Act on Measures against Alcohol-Related Health Harm and Contemporary Society," in *Creating Practical Sociology*, Chapter 2, Section 3, Japan Educational Foundation Publishing Bureau, 74–79.

Wakabayashi, M. and S. Ikoma (2020) "Earthquake Disaster and Alcohol-Related Problems," in Hirono, K. and K. Yaguchi ed. *10 years since the Great East Japan Earthquake: Analysis of Issues in Regeneration and Development—From the Perspective of Economic Analysis and Mental Care*, Chapter 6, Taisei-Shuppan, 114–137.

Wakabayashi, M. (2024) "Support for Alcohol-Related Problems after the Great East Japan Earthquake and the Situation 12 years Later: Focusing on Fukushima, Miyagi, and Iwate Prefectures," *Study of Mental Health and Social Welfare,* 30–38.

Chapter 5
Amount and the Method of Financial Support to Improve Earthquake-Proof Conversions of Rental Housing

Keiko Nosse Hirono

Abstract The collapse of non-earthquake-proof houses during severe seismic events results in casualties and hampers firefighting efforts, underscoring the imperative of formulating policies to enhance the earthquake resilience of rental properties. This study proposes a method to estimate the required financial support for improvements and compares the efficacy of tax incentives versus subsidies for promoting earthquake-proof conversions of rental housing for the first time. Combining the contingent valuation method and the discounted cash flow method, the study develops a model to examine consumers' evaluation of earthquake-proof conversions of rental houses and determines a rental firm's profits following such conversions. Application of these methods to analyze rental apartments in Tokyo and Miyagi Prefecture reveals that tenants are willing to pay less than 3000 yen/month in addition to their present rents for earthquake-proofing measures. This amount falls short of ensuring profitability for rental firms, emphasizing the necessity of financial support to bolster earthquake resilience in rental housing in Japan. Drawing from this analysis, the study proposes a method to determine the requisite financial support for earthquake-proof conversions, evaluating the merits of municipal fixed property tax reduction versus subsidy provision. The findings offer valuable insights for policymakers, informing strategies to incentive earthquake-proof conversions and enhance disaster preparedness in housing sector.

Keywords Earthquake · Housing policy · CVM · Willingness to pay · Earthquake-proof houses · Fixed property tax · Subsidy

K. N. Hirono (✉)
College of Economics, Nihon University, Chiyoda-ku, Tokyo, Japan
e-mail: hirono.keiko@nihon-u.ac.jp

K. N. Hirono, K. Yaguchi (eds.), *Reconstruction Period and the Stages of Regeneration After a Great Earthquake*, New Frontiers in Regional Science: Asian Perspectives 83, https://doi.org/10.1007/978-981-96-8822-7_5

5.1 Introduction

In 2011, the Great East Japan Earthquake devastated 127,800 houses and partially destroyed 275,807 more, resulting in significant loss of life (Taniguchi 2016). Given Japan's susceptibility to frequent seismic activity, earthquake-proof houses are necessary to mitigate the impact of earthquakes and reduce human and material losses. Enhancing the seismic resilience of rental properties is important for improving the quality of life and securing lives of inhabitants. Thus, formulating policies to ensure earthquake-proof rental housing is crucial. According to a survey by Sato (2018), 20.9% of houses in Japan lack earthquake-proofing, with the implementation rate of earthquake-proof conversion being only 2.1%.

In this chapter, I present a comprehensive approach to assessing earthquake-proof conversions in rental housing. Firstly, I develop a method to examine consumers' evaluation of such conversions. Secondly, I outline a framework for assessing a rental firm's profitability in implementing earthquake-proof construction work. Thirdly, based on the above analysis, I propose a method to determine the financial support needed for earthquake-proof conversions. Fourthly, using data on rental apartments in Tokyo and Miyagi Prefecture, I estimate consumers' willingness to pay for earthquake-proof conversions. I also estimate rental firms' profits from and the necessary financial assistance for earthquake-proof conversions of rental houses. Fifthly, I analyze the better form of financial support from the local government—tax reduction or subsidy. I assume a perfect competitive rental housing market with free entry. Firms enter this rental housing market—the market for earthquake-proof rental housing—if they can earn profits from earthquake-proof conversions of rental houses. The focus on earthquake-proof conversion of apartments is justified based on the following reasons. First, less than 30% of local governments subsidize earthquake-proof conversions of apartments. Second, non-earthquake-proof apartments account for 17.01% and 22.26% of wooden and non-wooden apartments, respectively (calculated using data from the Statistics Bureau, Ministry of Internal Affairs and Communications (2017)), indicating a significant number of non-earthquake-proof apartments. Third, apartments are homogeneous compared to detached houses, ensuring the accuracy of outcome of the analysis.

The contingent valuation method utilized in this chapter relies on the homogeneity of the analyzed houses' attributes. The lack of homogeneity could introduce partial–overall bias, as tenants' willingness to pay may vary depending on their perception of the houses' qualities. Specifically, relative to apartments, detached houses vary by layout, leading to differences in consumers' perceptions of houses. Consequently, asking about the willingness to pay for earthquake-proof conversions of detached houses could yield divergent responses, introducing bias and reducing the accuracy of the outcome. Hence, this chapter exclusively focuses on rental housing, specifically rental apartments.

This study centers on the earthquake-proof conversion of rental apartments for several reasons. Firstly, firms engaged in renting houses undertake earthquake-proof conversion projects only if they generate positive net profits. Financial support can bridge the gap between the project's costs and profits, facilitating project advancement. Conversely, individually owned houses may remain unconverted if owners fail to recognize the need for earthquake-proof housing, lack the time to execute the conversions (including the time to consult the constructor), lack information about seismic reinforcement and the right contractor, or face financial constraints. Secondly, non-earthquake-proof houses pose the risk of collapse during severe seismic events, jeopardizing the safety of inhabitants, neighbors, and passersby. Leveraging the expertise of housing companies can efficiently address these risks. Thus, the analysis focuses on rental housing managed by housing companies.

Notably, the earthquake-proof conversion of rental apartments has not progressed smoothly, primarily because rental companies fail to obtain expected returns from these projects. In this context, I aim to estimate consumers' willingness to pay for the earthquake-proof conversion of rental apartments and propose a method to determine whether undertaking these conversions is profitable for companies. I also present a method to assess whether and how much financial assistance is required for earthquake-proof conversions of rental apartments. I apply these methods to analyze rental apartments in the Tokyo Metropolitan Area and Miyagi Prefecture. Specifically, using the contingent valuation method, I calculate the additional rent consumers are willing to pay when rental companies earthquake proof their apartments. Using the outcome of this estimation and the discounted cash flow (DCF) method, I determine whether rental companies can generate profits from these conversions. If the projected profits fall short of covering the costs, the method proposed in this chapter enables local governments to determine the necessary financial support to accelerate earthquake-proof conversions of rental apartments.[1] I compare tax reduction and subsidy provision as a method of financial support both theoretically and practically.

Alonzo (2002) employs the contingent valuation method (CVM) to estimate consumers' willingness to pay for the benefits of barrier-free housing in Madrid and Barcelona. Sato et al. (2005) use CVM to analyze the demand and willingness to pay for barrier-free housing in the Tokushima Prefecture. Although Sato and Tamamura (2006) also apply CVM to evaluate earthquake-proof conversion of houses, their study differs from this chapter in the following ways. Firstly, Sato and Tamamura (2006) primarily analyze owner-occupied detached houses, whereas this chapter investigates rental apartments, including those in disaster-prone areas affected by the Great East Japan Earthquake, which provides a context for using the experience from the Great East Japan Earthquake. Secondly, unlike Sato and Tamamura (2006), this chapter incorporates the level of earthquake-proofing of houses into the willingness to pay question, defining earthquake-proof conversion as the level necessary to withstand an earthquake with a seismic intensity of seven on the Japanese seven-stage seismic scale, because the willingness to pay for the earthquake-proof conversion depends on the level of earthquake-proofing in the

[1] Refer to Hirono (2019) about the CVM and DCF methods in general. Hirono (2019) presents the method to calculate consumers' evaluation of the earthquake-proof conversion of housing. Data and a part of the analysis in this chapter are from Hirono (2020a, 2020b, 2022).

house. Thirdly, this chapter not only calculates consumers' willingness to pay for the earthquake-proof conversion of rental apartments using CVM but also estimates whether companies can earn profits from such conversions by combining the DCF method with CVM. Moreover, this chapter figures out the amount of financial support necessary for the earthquake-proof conversion of rental housing.

Yamaga et al. (2002) present pioneering study on earthquake-proof houses, which estimates the hedonic function of rents, demonstrating the difference in rents between rental apartments constructed according to earthquake-resistant design standards set before and after 1981 in Tokyo. They also determine the profitability of earthquake-proof conversions of houses.

This study differs from that of Yamaga et al. (2002) in several aspects. Firstly, this study does not adopt the earthquake-resistant design standards set after 1981 because houses conforming to this standard have been damaged by earthquake with a seismic intensity of seven. Secondly, this study considers not only Tokyo but also Miyagi Prefecture, one of the disaster areas of the Great East Japan Earthquake. Thirdly, while Yamaga et al. (2002) calculate the increment in rent from earthquake-proof conversions using the hedonic rent function, this study uses CVM. This can be attributed to the lack of data indicating whether each rental house can withstand an earthquake with a seismic intensity of seven, necessary for estimating rents using the hedonic rent function. Fourthly, this study presents the way to figure out the rental firms' profits from earthquake-conversion of rental apartments. Fifthly, this study introduces a method to calculate the financial support required for earthquake-proof conversions of rental apartments. Moreover, it discusses, for the first time, the comparison between tax reduction and local government subsidies to promote earthquake-proofing, both theoretically and practically.

This study, including Hirono (2020a, b, 2022), is the first to analyze several key points. First, using the CVM it estimates consumers' willingness to pay for earthquake-proof conversions of rental apartments to withstand seismic events with an intensity of seven. This willingness to pay reflects consumers' evaluation of such conversions. Second, this study constructs a model to compute the rental firms' profits from earthquake-proof conversions of rental apartments by integrating the CVM and the DCF method. Third, it determines consumers' willingness to pay for and the rental firms' profits from earthquake-resistant construction in the Tokyo Metropolitan Area and Miyagi Prefecture. Fourth, it develops a framework to determine the need for and amount of financial support from the local government. A novelty of this chapter is that, this chapter compares tax breaks and subsidies as methods of financial support. Our comparative analysis of different methods of financial support offers insights into effective policy implications for local governments to incentivize earthquake-proofing efforts among rental firms.

The remainder of the chapter is organized as follows. Section 5.2 presents the data and methods used in the analysis. Section 5.3 reports and interprets the analysis results as to consumers' willingness to pay for and firms' profits of earthquake-proof conversion of rental apartments. Section 5.4 proposes a method to calculate the amount of financial support required to accelerate earthquake-proof conversions of rental housing and formulates a financial support system applicable to local governments in general. Section 5.5 analyzes whether a tax break or subsidy is a superior method for improving earthquake-proof conversions of rental housing. Section 5.6 presents the conclusions.

5.2 Method of Analysis and Data

5.2.1 *Discounted Cash Flow Method*

This chapter adopts the DCF method as an investment criterion for the earthquake-proof conversion of houses. According to the DCF method, if the net present value (*NPV*) is positive, then the earthquake-proof conversion of rental housing will be profitable, and if the *NPV* is negative, then it will not be profitable. The *NPV* equals to the difference between the discounted present value of the present and future cash flows minus the cost of the earthquake-proof conversion of rental houses, where the cash flows are the increments in the rent created by the conversion.

The equations are expressed as follows. I assume that a company renting a house conducts the earthquake-proof conversion of rental housing. Denoting increment in the annual rent by X yen, the discount rate by r %, and the remaining useful life of the house by n, the discounted present value Q can be stated as

$$Q = X/(1+r) + X/(1+r)^2 + \cdots + X/(1+r)^n. \tag{5.1}$$

Since the *NPV* equals to the discounted present value of the present and future increments in the rent minus the cost, the *NPV* of the earthquake-proof conversion of this rental house is

$$NPV = X/(1+r) + X/(1+r)^2 + \cdots + X/(1+r)^n - C, \tag{5.2}$$

where C is the cost of the earthquake-proof conversions. I assume that *Xs* remain constant for all the periods.

I assume that the rental housing market is characterized by perfect competition with free entry. The rental firms conduct the earthquake-proof conversion of rental houses and enter the market if the *NPV* is positive, that is, when the earthquake-proof conversion is profitable.

5.2.2 *Contingent Valuation Method*

This chapter applies the contingent valuation method (CVM) to estimate the additional rent paid by consumers for the earthquake-proof conversion of rental apartments. Specifically, I use the CVM to calculate X in Eq. (5.2), which presents the formula to calculate the *NPV* of the earthquake-proof conversion of a rental apartment.

The CVM is employed to ask consumers their willingness to pay for an improvement in the level of goods not traded in the market (non-market goods), after explaining the consumers the contents of that good (Hidano 1999).

Ciriacy-Wantrup (1947) introduces the concept of CVM, in the United States, in 1947. Subsequently, in 1963, in an analysis, Davis (1963) pioneers the application of the CVM to the value of outdoor recreation in woods (Kuriyama 1998; Hidano 1999). In the 1980s, the application of CVM increased in the studies of the other countries. Concerning the theoretical analysis of CVM, Hanemann (1984) introduces a random utility model, and Cameron (1988) proposes a model based on the willingness to pay. Duffield and Patterson (1991) present a non-parametric approach without assuming a distribution function. With these theoretical backgrounds, CVM became the most used method in the evaluation of non-market goods. The CVM has application in a wide range of analysis, and not only for evaluating the ecosystem or the value of tropical forest.

The scope of CVM's application has become wider. It has been used in recent empirical studies in the fields of medicine (Taylor et al. 2010; Yokochi et al. 2014), criminology (Cohen et al. 2004), stadium construction (Ruszkowski 2017), and autonomous driving functions (Morita and Managi 2018). These applications of CVM are aimed at determining the value of non-traded products.

Concerning the field of construction, Alonzo (2002) applies CVM to barrier-free housing. In this context, it must be noted that the conditions for market existence are price and the volume demanded by the consumers; however, it is difficult to observe the price of being barrier-free. In this case, the price is determined by how much more consumers pay for barrier-free than non-barrier-free housing. Since this additional price cannot be observed, there is no market for the barrier-free quality of a house (Alonzo 2002). Hence, Alonzo (2002) applies CVM to determine the pricing for barrier-free housing. Similarly, there is no market for the earthquake-proof conversion of rental houses. In most cases, the advertising catalogs and listings in housing advertisement magazines fail to provide information about whether a rental house is earthquake proof. This keeps consumers from knowing the rent appraisal for the earthquake-proofed rental houses—the difference between the rental price of an earthquake-proofed house and that of a non-earthquake-proofed house. Since this rental price cannot be observed or captured by consumers, there is no market for the earthquake-proof conversion of rental house. Although price has aspects of an evaluation of the goods and services, rental companies cannot grasp evaluation of the earthquake-proof conversion and its price, that is, an increment in the rent for the earthquake-proof conversion of the rental house. Therefore, it is appropriate to use CVM to estimate the rent appraisal for the earthquake-proofed rental houses.

5.2.3 Procedure of Estimation

In this research, I calculate X in Eqs. (5.1) and (5.2), by adopting CVM. I use the data on rental apartments in the Tokyo metropolitan area and the Miyagi Prefecture. The Miyagi Prefecture includes the disaster area of an earthquake with a seismic intensity of seven. Specifically, by using the questionnaire survey in Sect. 5.2.4, I ask the consumers their willingness to pay for the earthquake-proof conversion of rental apartments. Subsequently, by applying the DCF method, I estimate the *NPV* of the future increment in rent due to the earthquake-proof conversion. If the *NPV* has a positive sign, then the rental companies will carry out the construction work. Conversely, if the *NPV* is negative, there would be a need for governments' financial support to accelerate the conversion. Given this, if the *NPV* has a negative sign, then the amount of financial support should be at least the absolute value of the *NPV*.

5.2.4 Questionnaire Survey on the Earthquake-Proof Conversion of Rental Apartments

1. **Sampled Period and Respondents**

   The questionnaire survey on the earthquake-proof conversion of rental apartments covers the period from February 3–7, 2017. The respondents of the questionnaire are the tenants of the apartments in Tokyo and the Miyagi Prefecture, whose commuting time from the center of the prefectures (Tokyo and Sendai stations, respectively) is less than 1.5 h. I restrict the sample to respondents with a personal income and aged between 20 and 70 years.[2] This is because the survey takes the payment of rental by the respondents into account.

   I analyze the Miyagi Prefecture because it is the only prefecture hit by an earthquake of a seismic intensity of seven in the Great East Japan Earthquake. I also analyze Tokyo because consumers' attitude toward the earthquake-proof conversion may depend on whether the prefecture is in the disaster-stricken area. Another reason for choosing Tokyo is the high income of residents in Tokyo, relative to those in the Miyagi Prefecture, given that the income of residents may influence their willingness to pay for the earthquake-proof conversion of rental houses.

   Here, I assume the model of a monocentric city. In other words, I presume that the housing market expands around the center of the city—the Tokyo and Sendai stations for the Tokyo and Miyagi Prefectures, respectively. According to Hirono (2004), the region requiring residents to take more than 90 min of commute to the city's center constitutes a different housing market. The consumers of this market emphasize different attributes of rental houses (from the attributes which consumers whose commuting time of less than 1.5 h to the center of the city think most important when choosing a rental home). Therefore, I choose respondents whose commuting time to the center of the city is less than 1.5 h.

   The survey is carried out online by a research company. Although an online questionnaire survey may be disadvantageous in collecting responses from respondents aged over 70 years, the survey helped in collecting sufficient correct responses from respondents of this age group.

---

[2] The respondents in the seventies age group earn a pension which is a kind of personal income. Thus, I include this age group in the questionnaire.

As this chapter is based on the online questionnaire survey, the respondents were registered as questionnaire monitors in the research company. The sampling method is purposive sampling. The population of this survey is those who live in rental housing in Tokyo and Miyagi Prefecture.

The questionnaire survey has 186 active parts (100 and 86 in Tokyo and the Miyagi Prefecture, respectively). I manage the sampling in such a manner that the proportion of the elderly and household income match those of the population, given that these aspects seemed to have relevance to the willingness to pay for the earthquake-proof conversion of rental housing. I match the proportion of the elderly with that of the population. For non-random selection, I set the proportion of respondents above 60 years to 30%, which is same as the proportion in the rental housing data collected by the Statistic Bureau of Ministry of Internal Affairs and Communications (2017). Concerning the household income, I set the distribution ratio of sampling according to the Ministry of Land, Infrastructure, Transport and Tourism (MLIT) (2017). For example, the tenants with a household income of 4–6 million yen account for 27.4% of the respondents in this data and 26.9% in MLIT (2017). The proportion of tenants with a household income of 6–8 million yen represent 14.5% of the respondents in this data and 13.3% in MLIT (2017). The proportion of tenants earning 8–10 million yen represent 6.5% in this data and 5.7% in MLIT (2017).

2. **Content of the Questionnaire**

   First, I collect the demographic details of the respondents—age, gender, household income, and the place of residence. I also enquire about the type of house in which they live—rental or owned house, wooden or non-wooden apartment, or a detached house—and their experience of an earthquake with a seismic intensity of above 6 in the previous 10 years. Second, I ask them the need of earthquake-proof conversion of rental houses to withstand an earthquake with a seismic intensity of seven. This question intended to gauge respondents' awareness of the need for the earthquake-proof conversion of rental homes. Finally, I ask about the consumers' willingness to pay for the earthquake-proof conversion of rental houses.

3. **Attributes of the Respondents**

   Among the respondents, male and female respondents comprise 50.54% (94 people) and 49.46% (92 people), respectively. The highest proportion of respondents is in the thirties, accounting for 27.42% (51 people), followed by 26.34% (49 people) respondents in the sixties (see Fig. 5.1). Concerning the household income, the proportion of households earning 2–4 million yen is the largest at 37.63% (70 people), followed by 27.42% (51 people) households with an income of 4–6 million yen (see Fig. 5.2). The respondents with an experience of an earthquake with a seismic intensity of above 6, in the previous 10 years, represent 50% (93 people) of the respondents.

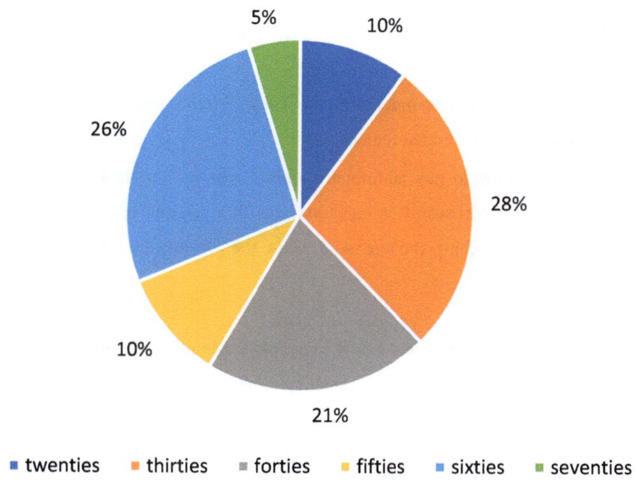

Fig. 5.1 Age of the respondents

Fig. 5.2 Household income of the respondents

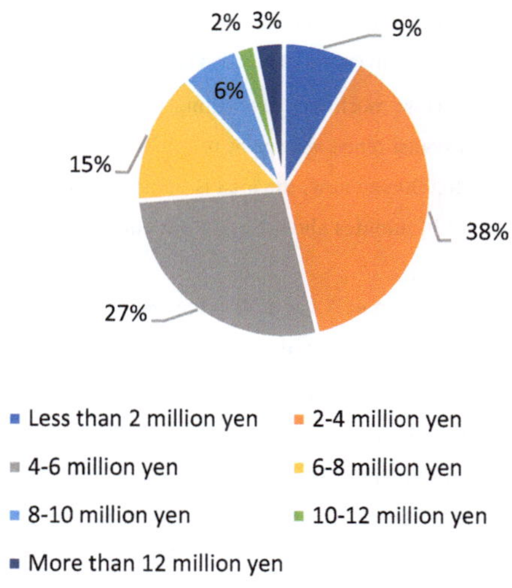

4. **Questions on the Willingness to Pay**

I formulate four types of questions on the willingness to pay for the earthquake-proof conversion of rental houses, as shown in Fig. 5.3. I ask the residents of Tokyo about wooden (Question 1) and non-wooden (Question 2) apartments. I ask the residents of the Miyagi Prefecture the questions about wooden (Question 3) and non-wooden apartments (Question 4), respectively.

The choices of the willingness to pay are 0 yen, 1 ~ 499 yen, 500 ~ 999 yen, 1000 ~ 1499 yen, 1500 ~ 1999 yen, 2000 ~ 2499 yen, 2500 ~ 2999 yen, 3000 ~ 3499 yen, 3500 ~ 3999 yen, 4000 ~ 4499 yen, 4500 ~ 4999 yen, 5000 ~ 5499 yen, 5500 ~ 5999 yen, 6000 ~ 6499 yen, 6500 ~ 6999 yen, 7000 ~ 7499 yen, 7500 ~ 7999 yen, 8000 ~ 8499 yen, 8500 ~ 8999, 9000 ~ 9499

Figure 5.3 Questions about evaluation of earthquake-proof conversion of rental apartment

(Question 1: A question to the respondents in the Tokyo Metropolitan area about evaluation of earthquake-proof conversion of wooden rental apartment)

How much are you willing to pay additional monthly rent for earthquake-proof conversion of wooden rental apartment to withstand an earthquake with a seismic intensity of seven. Rent is 63,000 yen now, the area is 27 m^2, the age is 23 years, the commuting time to the Tokyo station is 39 minutes about this apartment.

(Question 2: A question to the respondents in the Tokyo Metropolitan area about evaluation of earthquake-proof conversion of non- wooden rental apartment)

How much are you willing to pay additional monthly rent for earthquake-proof conversion of non-wooden (Steel-reinforced concrete structure or steel structure) rental apartment to withstand an earthquake with a seismic intensity of seven. Rent is 90,000 yen now, the area is 37 m^2, the age is 18 years, the commuting time to the Tokyo station is 39 minutes about this apartment.

(Question 3: A question to the respondents in the Miyagi Prefecture about evaluation of earthquake-proof conversion of wooden rental apartment)

How much are you willing to pay additional monthly rent for earthquake-proof conversion of wooden rental apartment to withstand an earthquake with a seismic intensity of seven. Rent is 46,000 yen now, the area is 35 m^2, the age is 17 years, the commuting time to the Sendai station is 24 minutes about this apartment.

(Question 4: A question to the respondents in the Miyagi Prefecture about evaluation of earthquake-proof conversion of non- wooden rental apartment)

How much are you willing to pay additional monthly rent for earthquake-proof conversion of non-wooden (Steel-reinforced concrete structure or steel structure) rental apartment to withstand an earthquake with a seismic intensity of seven. Rent is 55,000 yen now, the area is 39 m^2, the age is 17 years, the commuting time to the Sendai station is 24 minutes about this apartment.

Fig. 5.3 Questions about evaluation of earthquake-proof conversion of rental apartment

yen, 9500 ~ 9999 yen, and more than 10,000 yen. I ask the respondents to choose one of these ranges. Specifically, I ask the respondents the additional amount of rent they will pay for the earthquake-proof conversions of rental apartments. I present the choices in the units of 500 yen because of the following reasons. *Forento* (a Japanese rental housing magazine) lists most of the rents in the units of 1000 yen or 10,000 yen. In the Japanese rental housing market, rents are set in the units of 1000 yen or 10,000 yen, and consumers' expectation of rents corresponds to these units. However, the rents of a few rental houses are listed in the units of 500 yen such as 95,500 yen. Thus, concerning the choices provided in the questionnaire, the price range is set narrowly using the units of 500 yen to avoid leakage.

Let X be the average value of the willingness to pay for the earthquake-proof conversions of rental apartments (i.e., answer to questions in Fig. 5.3). Using this X, I calculate the *NPV* for this conversion in Eq. (5.2).

Concerning the area, the building's age, and the commuting time, in Questions 1–4 in Fig. 5.3, I use the average value of those (the area, the building's age, and the commuting time) of the wooden and non-wooden private rental apartments in Tokyo and the Miyagi Prefecture, respectively, from the data provided by the Statistic Bureau of Ministry of Internal Affairs and Communications (MIC) (2017). As for the rents in Fig. 5.3, I use the monthly rent data provided by MIC (2017) for wooden and non-wooden private apartments in Tokyo and the Miyagi Prefecture.

Concerning the earthquake-proof level, some studies determine whether the houses are earthquake proof based on the new seismic code for houses set in 1981. However, I define the earthquake-resisting performance of houses based on whether houses can resist earthquakes with a seismic intensity of seven. Therefore, I ask about the willingness to pay rent for conversions that help rental apartments resist earthquakes with a seismic intensity of seven. This is because houses built based on the new seismic code can resist only earthquakes with a seismic intensity of 6; thus, the new seismic code falls short as a seismic code. For example, the Great Hanshin-Awaji Earthquake with a seismic intensity of seven caused complete and medium or small damage to 8.6% and 16.7%, respectively, of the buildings conforming to the new seismic code (Yoshizawa Architectural Structure Design 2013). Thus, I define the earthquake-resistant houses as houses that can resist earthquakes with a seismic intensity of seven, which is the highest earthquake scale.

I set the quality of rental houses in terms of the area, building age, commuting time to the city center, and the type of apartment (wooden or non-wooden house), in Questions 1–4 in Fig. 5.3.[3] This approach allows the respondents to capture the concrete image of the rental house in the question. I ask the respondents their willingness to pay for these rental houses with the specified quality, because the CVM is the method to ask the consumers their willingness to pay for goods or services of a certain quality. For instance, if I use the general word in the question house, which includes all the houses, such as apartments, detached house, wooden and non-wooden house, then there would be a significant variance in the respondents' willingness to pay (see Fig. 5.3).

[3] The prices of the apartments depend only on the area, the age of the apartments, the commuting time to the city center, if construction of the apartments is same (Hirono 2004). Thus, in the question on the willingness to pay, I set these as the quality parameters of a house.

5.2.5 Data

In this chapter, I determine the profitability of the earthquake-proof conversion of rental housing by estimating Eq. (5.2). In this procedure, as the discount rate, I use the real interest rate on 10-year government bonds.[4]

To calculate Eq. (5.2), I set the lifespan of housing as 32.2 years, based on the research by MLIT (1996). The remaining useful life of the house n—the period for which the future additional rents for earthquake-proof conversion is discounted—is calculated by the lifespan of housing minus the average age of housing. I calculated this period as for the wooden and non-wooden rental apartments in Tokyo and the Miyagi Prefecture, respectively. I set the cost of making the rental houses earthquake proof at 50,000 yen/m^2, which is the average of the data in the earthquake countermeasure website called Taishin Net (2017).[5] I calculate the cost of earthquake-proof conversion of rental houses in Tokyo and Miyagi by multiplying rental apartments' average area (in each prefecture) by 50,000 yen.

The data used in this chapter are the respondents' willingness to pay for the earthquake-proof conversion of rental housing X and the NPV also.

5.3 Outcome of Analysis

5.3.1 Awareness of the Earthquake-Proof Conversion of Housing

Firstly, based on the outcome of the questionnaire survey, I present consumers' perception of the need of earthquake-proof conversion of rental housing (see Fig. 5.4).

According to Fig. 5.4, 84% of the consumers were aware of the need for making rental houses resistant to earthquakes with a seismic intensity of seven. Overall, consumers strongly felt the need for earthquake-proof rental housing.

[4] By denoting the inflation rate as π and nominal interest rate m, the value of 1 yen will be $1 + m\text{-}\pi$ yen, that is, the value of money will decrease by inflation. Hence, I set the real interest rate as the discount rate. I use the real interest rate on 10-year government bonds as the discount rate, because the long-term investment is required for earthquake-proofing rental houses.

[5] The tenant-occupied rental houses can be made earthquake proof using the following methods: fitting steel frame into the walls of the house from the corridor, reinforcing using a strong structure, and out framing (fitting steel frame from outside of the building) (New Japan Reform 2019).

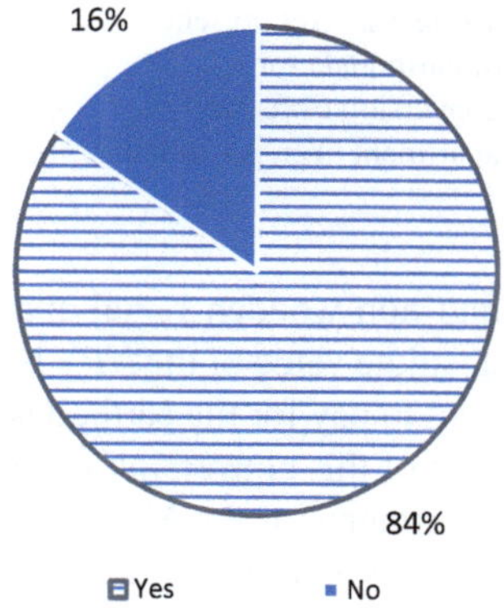

Fig. 5.4 The need for earthquake-proof conversion of rental housing

Table 5.1 The willingness to pay for construction work to make rental houses earthquake-proof (Yen per month)

	Tokyo metropolitan area	Miyagi prefecture
Wooden	2,705	2,267
Non-wooden	2,786	2,090

5.3.2 Profitability of Earthquake-Proof Conversion of Rental Houses

Next, I provide the average willingness to pay an additional rent for the earthquake-proof conversion of rental houses such that the houses can withstand earthquakes with a seismic intensity of seven. Table 5.1 shows this willingness to pay—the average value of the willingness to pay for the earthquake-proof conversions of rental apartments (i.e., answer to questions in Fig. 5.3). Specifically, Table 5.1 shows the willingness to pay for the wooden and non-wooden apartments both in the Tokyo metropolitan area and Miyagi Prefecture (see Table 5.1). The figures in Table 5.1 times 12 correspond to *X* in Eqs. (5.1) and (5.2).

The above finding shows that although 84% of the consumers express the need for the earthquake-proof conversion of rental houses, they are willing to pay only 2800 yen/month additionally for this conversion. In other words, there exists a gap between consumers' awareness of earthquake-proof conversion of rental houses and their willingness to pay an additional rent for the conversion. As stated earlier, I estimate the *NPV* to determine the profits from this conversion.

I use the average value of the willingness to pay *X*, from Table 5.1; I collect data on the lifespan of housing and use the figure of the discount rate and the cost of earthquake-proofing in Sect. 5.2.5. Based on the results of these estimations, I calculate the *NPV* of the earthquake-proof conversion of rental apartments (see Table 5.2).

The earthquake-proof conversion of rental apartments has been less profitable in the Miyagi Prefecture than that in the Tokyo metropolitan area for both the wooden

Table 5.2 Net present value of earthquake-proof conversion of rental apartment (Yen per month)

	Tokyo metropolitan area	Miyagi prefecture
Wooden	−1,053,839	−1,342,313
Non-wooden	−1,381,308	−1,574,197

and non-wooden rental apartments. In other words, the *NPV* is negative, and the absolute value of the *NPV* is larger. This can be attributed to the fact that the willingness to pay for the earthquake-proof conversion of rental housing is smaller, and the cost of this conversion is higher. Higher cost reflects that the average area of rental apartments in the Miyagi Prefecture is larger than that of the Tokyo Metropolitan area. In both prefectures, the non-wooden rental apartments are less profitable than that of the wooden rental apartments; this can be attributed to the larger area and higher cost of non-wooden rental apartments.

Overall, Table 5.2 indicates that the earthquake-proof conversion of rental housing is not profitable for rental firms. The outcome of *NPV* does not reveal an incentive for rental firms to make existing rental apartments earthquake proof and enter the market of earthquake-proof rental housing.

5.4 The Method of Financial Support to Accelerate Earthquake-Proof Conversions of Rental Apartments

This section proposes a method to estimate the amount of financial support necessary for earthquake-proof conversions of rental apartments, based on examples from Miyagi Prefecture and the Tokyo Metropolitan Area as policy implications. Additionally, it outlines a plan for the formulation of local government financial support for such conversions.

1. **Need for Financial Support**

As earthquake-proof conversions of rental houses have proven unprofitable for rental firms, providing financial support to expedite this construction work is necessary. Governments should offer this support for the following reasons. Firstly, safeguarding inhabitants' lives from earthquakes is crucial. Secondly, non-earthquake-proof rental apartments have witnessed a twofold increase in the percentage of fires caused by their collapses during severe earthquakes, resulting in a decline in early fire extinguishing efforts by inhabitants (MLIT 2000). Collapses and fires in rental apartments pose life-threatening risks not only for inhabitants but also for neighborhoods and passersby. Thirdly, the collapse of rental apartments causes road blockades, obstructing the passage of relief vehicles and fire engines.

2. **Amount of Financial Support**

The amount of financial support is set to incentivize rental firms to undertake earthquake-proof conversions of rental apartments. This support aims to ensure that earthquake-proofing projects yield positive *NPV*, motivating rental firms to execute projects and enter the earthquake-proof rental housing market. To expedite earthquake-proof conversions of rental apartments, the financial support should bridge the gap between expected profits and costs. Specifically, the amount of financial support should be at least the absolute value of the discounted present value of the present and future increments in rent minus the cost (as illustrated in Table 5.2). Overall, the per unit amount of financial support for wooden and non-wooden apartments should be 1,053,839 yen and 1,381,308 yen, in the Tokyo Metropolitan Area and 1,342,313 yen and 1,574,197 yen in Miyagi Prefecture, respectively.

3. **Method to Determine the Need for and the Amount of Financial Support**

Any local government can adopt the above method to estimate the amount of financial support required to accelerate earthquake-proof conversions of rental apartments in the Tokyo Metropolitan Area and Miyagi Prefecture. This method assesses whether and how much financial support rental firms require. If a rental firm qualifies to receive financial support, the amount is calculated based on the firm's need.

This method involves the following steps. First, using the CVM, I calculate the consumers' willingness to pay for earthquake-proof conversions of rental apartments. Second, using the outcome of the willingness to pay, I assess the need for financial support according to rental firms' *NPV*, which is calculated using the DCF method. A negative *NPV* indicates the unprofitability of an earthquake-proofing project and highlights the need for financial support. I compute the minimum amount of financial support as the absolute value of *NPV*.

4. **Source of Financial Support**

For the source of financial support, I first propose a subsidy from local governments, because inhabitants' lives form the top priority of local government subsidies (Hirono 2020a). Second, I suggest a reduction in the fixed property tax on earthquake-proof rental housing, which can facilitate earthquake-proof conversion projects. The amount of assistance through subsidy or tax reduction can be calculated using the method outlined in 3. above. In the next section, I compare the reduction in fixed property tax and subsidies from both theoretical and practical viewpoints. Note that both the reduction in the fixed property tax and subsidies from the local government rely on the budget of the local government, because the fixed property tax is levied by the local government.

5.5 Comparison Between Fixed Property Tax Reduction and Subsidy Provision

In comparing fixed property tax reduction with subsidy provision for earthquake-proof rental housing, we can analyze theoretically by examining the deadweight loss associated with each scenario. In Fig. 5.5, D is the demand curve of earthquake-proof rental housing, While S is the supply curve of such housing when neither fixed property tax nor subsidy is applied. E is the equilibrium in the market of

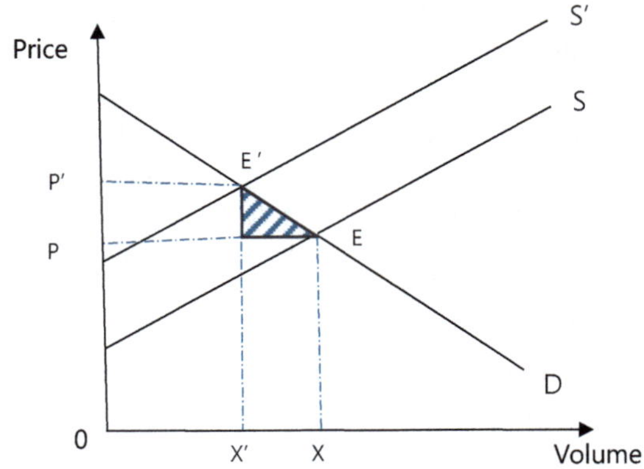

Fig. 5.5 Dead weight loss caused by fixed property tax

earthquake-proof rental housing under these conditions. Note that although a market for earthquake-proof conversions of rental housing does not exist, a market for earthquake-proof rental housing is indeed present.

However, the current reality in Japan is that fixed property tax is levied on each rental housing unit. To lend one more unit of a house, the supplier of earthquake-proof rental housing should pay the fixed property tax for that unit, which is included in the marginal cost of earthquake-proof rental housing. Thus, the market equilibrium is E′ as illustrated in Fig. 5.5. The reason is that marginal cost of earthquake-proof rental housing increases by the current amount of the fixed property tax per earthquake-proof rental housing unit, leading to a new supply curve, denoted as S′ instead of S. Therefore, the equilibrium of the current market for earthquake-proof rental housing is E′ instead of E. The imposition of fixed property tax results in a deadweight loss equivalent to the shaded area in Fig. 5.5 under the present situation (see Fig. 5.5).

If the fixed property tax on earthquake-proof rental housing is reduced, for once, the marginal cost per unit decreases accordingly. If the current amount of fixed property tax exceeds the reduced amount of fixed property tax, then the supply curve of earthquake-proof rental housing moves from S′ to S″ in Fig. 5.6. Consequently, the market equilibrium of earthquake-proof rental housing moves from E′ to E″ and the deadweight loss decreases to the shaded area in Fig. 5.6. The reduced amount of the fixed property tax should match the necessary amount calculated to accelerate earthquake-proof conversions of rental apartments, as discussed in Sect. 5.4.

Conversely, if the amount of current fixed property tax levied on earthquake-proof rental apartments is smaller than the reduction in the fixed property tax to expedite earthquake-proof conversions of rental apartments, the supply curve shifts from S′ to S″ (lower than S). The market equilibrium moves from E′ to E″ and the volume of earthquake-proof rental housing increases from X′ to X″. Although the deadweight loss caused by the current fixed property tax diminishes, a new deadweight loss, indicated by the shaded area in Fig. 5.7, appears.

In the case that a local government offers subsidies for earthquake-proof conversions of rental housing, the amount per unit should match the amount of fixed

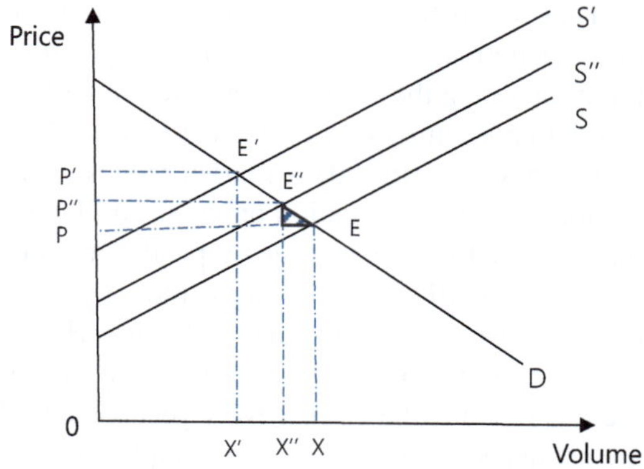

Fig. 5.6 Dead weight loss caused by financial support (the amount of financial support is less than the current amount of fixed property tax)

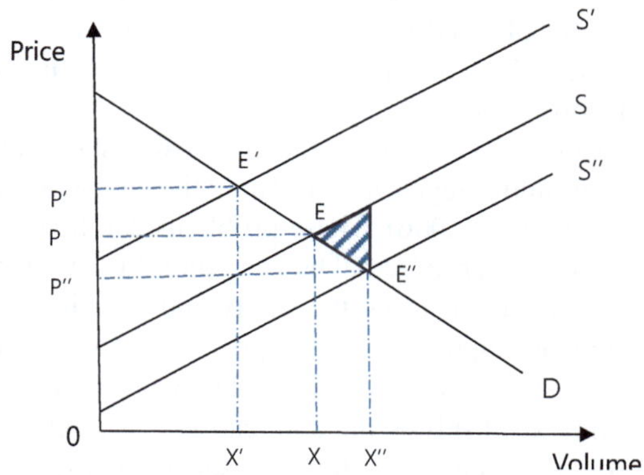

Fig. 5.7 Dead weight loss caused by financial support (the amount of financial support is larger than the current amount of fixed property tax)

property tax reduction mentioned above, because the former amount is necessary to make rental housing earthquake proof calculated by the way shown in Sect. 5.4. If the amount of current fixed property tax is larger than the amount of subsidy, the supply curve shifts from S′ to S″ because of the decrease in the marginal cost of the firm supplying earthquake-proof rental housing. The firm's marginal cost decreases because the subsidy reduces the cost of supplying one more unit of earthquake-proof rental housing. Consequently, the deadweight loss represented by the shaded area in Fig. 5.6 occurs. The extent of the supply curve shift from S′ to S″ matches that caused by the fixed property tax reduction, because the amount of subsidy per unit equals the tax reduction per unit of earthquake-proof rental housing (see Fig. 5.6).

If the amount of fixed property tax currently levied on earthquake-proof rental housing is smaller than the amount of subsidy, the supply curve shifts from S′ to S″ (lower than S), resulting in a deadweight loss represented by the shaded area in Fig. 5.7. The extent of the supply curve shift from S′ to S″ matches that caused by the fixed property tax reduction because the amount of subsidy per unit and tax reduction per unit of earthquake-proof rental housing are identical (see Fig. 5.7).

Thus, the theoretical effect of reducing fixed property tax and providing subsidies is identical. Consequently, the comparison now shifts to the operational viewpoint regarding the method of acceleration of earthquake-proof conversions.

On important issue with fixed property tax is that the assessed values of land and houses deviates from their market values. This discrepancy arises because of the complexity of the valuation process. The Japanese Government has acknowledged that assessed property values typically amount to approximately 70% of market values, with differences falling within 30% of market values deemed as evaluation errors rather than significant problems (Horikawa 2020). Additionally, land and houses of a specific quality may not even have available market prices because they are not traded in the market every year, Usually the market prices of land and prices are estimated values based on assumptions of trade (Yonehara 2001).

However, the proposal outlined in this chapter does not aim to alter the assessed values of the fixed property tax on land and houses but focuses on adjusting the amount of fixed property tax on earthquake-proof rental housing. Therefore, the shortcomings of the current property valuation system do not pose a hindrance to this proposal.

Conversely, problems with subsidies provided by local governments include uncertainties regarding their effectiveness and a lack of clarity on their actual condition (Oosugi 2006). These problems can be resolved by disclosing the number of earthquake-proof rental housing units built with subsidies, demonstrating the role of subsidies in ensuring the safety and security of inhabitants, and emphasizing that safeguarding lives is the top priority of local government subsidies (Hirono 2020a).

The practical problem of subsidy is that the initial and indispensable step in providing a subsidy is the application of suppliers (i.e., firms) seeking to earthquake proof their rental housing for a subsidy to the local government. Without such applications, subsidies cannot be granted, even if rental housing requires earthquake-proofing and subsidy assistance is available.

By contrast, fixed property tax is usually imposed on all rental properties within a local government's jurisdiction. Therefore, implementing a tax break for earthquake-proof rental housing can effectively benefit all eligible properties. Although the theoretical effect of fixed property tax breaks and local government subsidies on earthquake-proof rental housing is equivalent, in practice, the smooth increase in earthquake-proof rental housing can be achieved through the reduction in fixed property tax on such rental properties. Thus, the preferred method of financial support for improving earthquake-proof conversions of rental housing is to reduce the fixed property tax on earthquake-proof rental housing.

5.6 Conclusion

Although over 80% of the respondents expressed a need for earthquake-proof conversions of apartments, their willingness to pay was limited to less than 3000 yen/month in addition to the current rent for such conversions. For rental firms, this suggests that these construction projects would yield negative profits. This finding underscores the lack of progress in earthquake-proof conversions of rental apartments, highlighting the necessity for financial support to enhance the seismic resilience of housing and prevent the loss of human lives.

To address this issue, I devised a framework to calculate the amount of financial support that municipal governments could provide. This involved determining the disparity between the discounted present value of current and future cash flows and the costs associated with earthquake-proof conversions of rental housing, combining the CVM and the DCF method. This framework can be utilized in any municipal government financial support program for earthquake-proofing projects. Through this analysis, I demonstrated that the preferred method of financial support for enhancing the seismic resilience of rental housing is to reduce the fixed property tax on earthquake-proof rental housing, rather than a subsidy from the local government. Safeguarding of housing and inhabitants in the house by earthquake-conversion contributes to continuous development of the region.

References

Alonzo, F. (2002) "The Benefits of Building Barrier-free: A Contingent Valuation of Accessibility as an Attribute of Housing," *European Journal of Housing Policy*, 2(1), 25–44.

Cameron, T. A. (1988) "A New Paradigm for Valuing Non-market Goods Using Referendum Data: Maximum Likelihood Estimation by Censored Logistic Regression," *Journal of Environmental Economics and Management,* 15(3), 355–379.

Ciriacy-Wantrup, S. V. (1947) "Capital Returns from Soil-Conservation Practices," *Journal of Farm Economics*, 29, 1181–1196.

Cohen, M. A., R. T. Rust et al. (2004) "Willingness-to-pay for Crime Control Programs," *Criminology,* 42(1), 89–110.

Davis, R. K. (1963) "The Value of Outdoor Recreation: an Economic Study of Maine Woods," Unpublished Ph.D. dissertation, Harvard University, Cambridge, MA.

Duffield, J. W. and D. A. Patterson (1991) "Inference and Optimal Design for a Welfare Measure in Dichotomous Choice Contingent Valuation," *Land Economics,* 67(2), 225–239.

Hanemann, W. M. (1984) "Welfare Evaluations in Contingent Valuation Experiments with Discrete Responses," *American Journal of Agriculture Economics,* 66, 332–341.

Hidano, N. ed. (1999) *Kankyo to Gyosei no Keizaihyouka–CVM Manual– [Economic Evaluation of Environment and Administration: Manual of CVM],* Tokyo: Keiso Shobo.

Hirono, K. N. (2004) "Imperfect Information and the Amount of Housing Ownership," *Pacific Economic Review,* 9(4), 335–343.

Hirono, K. N. (2019) "Kasoshijouhou niyoru Jutaku no Hyouka [Evaluation of Housing Facility by the Contingent Valuation Method]," *Journal of Property Assessment Policy,* 19(2), 1–8.

Hirono, K. N. (2020a) "Jutaku no Taishinka ni Muketa Hojokin–Taishinka heno Shohisha no Shiharaiishigaku no Bunseki–[Subsidy to Make Housing Earthquake-Proof: An Analysis of Consumers' Willingness to Pay]," in Hirono, K. N. and K. Yaguchi ed., *Higashinihondaishinsai kara 10 nen: Saisei · hatten ni Okeru Kadai no Bunseki [Analysis on Reconstruction Period and the Stages of Regeneration after a Great Earthquake: Ten Years after Great East Japan Earthquake],* Tokyo: Taisei Shuppan.

Hirono, K. N. (2020b) "Chintaijutaku no Taishinka ni muketa Hojogaku no Suikei [A Method for Estimation of the Amount of Subsidy to Accelerate Earthquake-Proof Conversion of Rental Housing]," *Studies in Regional Science*, 50(1), 19–38.

Hirono, K. N. (2022) *Economic Analysis of Housing Policy in Japan: Policy Concerning Housing Quality,* Springer.

Horikawa, H. (2020) *Koteishisanhyouka Kaitaishinsho [Anatomical Book of Fixed Property Tax Evaluation],* Tokyo: Seiunsha.

Kuriyama, K. (1998) *Kankyo no Kachi to Hyoka no Shuho—CVM niyoru Keizaihyouka— [Value of Environment and a Method of Estimation],* Hokkaido University.

Ministry of Land, Infrastructure, Transport and Tourism (1996) *Construction White Paper.*

Ministry of Land, Infrastructure, Transport and Tourism (2000) *Taishinkaishusuishin Chosa no Kekkka [The Outcome of the Survey on Acceleration of Earthquake-Proof Conversion].*

Ministry of Land, Infrastructure, Transport and Tourism (2017) *Jutaku Shijo Doukou Chosa Houkokusho [A Report on the Survey of the Japanese Housing Market].*

Morita, T. and S. Managi (2018) "Model Comparisons on Estimating Willingness to Pay for Auto Driving Systems," (in Japanese), *Yamanashi Glocal Studies,* Yamanashi Prefectural University, No. 13, 71–80.

New Japan Reform (2019) *Earthquake-Resistant Construction of Buildings and Apartments,* (in Japanese). http://www.sn-reform.co.jp/reform/earthquakeproof/

Oosugi, S. (2006) "Jichitai-hojokinkaikaku to Gyoseihyoka no Kadai (Reform of Local Governments' Subsidy and Problems in Policy Evaluation)," *Kaikei-kensa Kenkyu,* Board of Audit of Japan, No. 33, 103–119.

Ruszkowski, R. (2017) "The Contingent Valuation Method in Assessing the Value of Sport's Stadium in Developing Nations. The Case of Poland," *MPRA Paper,* No. 80581, 1–20.

Sato, K. (2018) "Estimation of Housing Earthquake Resistant Rate Using Micro Data of Housing and Land Survey 2013," (in Japanese), *Research Paper,* No. 42, Statistical Research and Training Institute, Ministry of Internal Affairs and Communications.

Sato, K. and M. Tamamura (2006) "A Study on Resident Consciousness for Retrofitting of Existing Houses by Contingent Valuation Method: a Case study at Ichikawa City, Chiba Pref.," (in Japanese), *Journal of Social Safety Science,* No. 8, Institute of Social Safety Science, 81–87.

Sato, S., M. Kondo and K. Watanabe (2005) "Analysis of Demand for Barrier-free House and Effect in Reduction of Burden," (in Japanese), *Journal of Architecture and Planning,* No. 592, Architectural Institute of Japan, 193–199.

Statistics Bureau of Ministry of Internal Affairs and Communications (2017) *Results of 2013 Housing and Land Survey.*

Taishin Net (2017) *Initial Cost of Seismic Reinforcement,* (in Japanese). http://www.taisin-neto.com/solution/online_seminer/sindanhokyou/

Taniguchi, H. (2016) "Shinsai to Community [Earthquake and Communities]," in Maruo, N., K. Yaguchi and G. Miyagaki ed., *Community no Saisei [Regeneration of Communities],* Tokyo: Chuokeizai-sha.

Taylor, C. B., M. Stevenson, S. Jan, et al. (2010) "A Systematic Review of the Costs and Benefits of Helicopter Emergency Medical Services," *Injury,* 41, 10–20.

Yamaga, H., M. Nakagawa and M. Saito (2002) "Earthquake Risk and Rent: Political Implication for Earthquake Proof Countermeasure," (in Japanese), *JCER Economc Journal,* 46, 1–21.

Yokochi, M., T. Terashita and K. Ogasawara (2014) "Comparison of the Willingness to Pay for Air Ambulance between Three Regions Using CVM," (in Japanese), *Journal of the Japan Society for Healthcare Administration,* 51(1), 41–52.

Yonehara, J. (2001) "Koteisisanzei no Honshitsu to Kaikaku no Houkou (Essence and the Direction of Reform of Fixed Property Tax)," in Hashimoto T. ed., *Chihozei no Riron to Kadai [Theory and Problems of Local Taxes],* Zeimukeirikyokai.

Yoshizawa Architectural Structure Design (2013) *Tateru [Construct],* (in Japanese).

Chapter 6
Interregional Risk Sharing and Fiscal System for Natural Disasters

Naoki Sakamoto and Kazunori Nakajima

Abstract Income in a disaster-stricken area after a natural disaster decreases with the abandonment of capital stock and other factors, but income in non-disaster-stricken areas may increase because of a concentration of halted production. Similarly, income in disaster-stricken areas increases with investment in disaster prevention, recovery, and reconstruction to cope with natural disasters, but it is uncertain whether income increases or decreases in non-disaster-stricken areas. Thus, not only natural disasters but also investment in disaster prevention, recovery, and reconstruction has asymmetric spillover effects across regions. Based on these effects, this chapter theoretically examines interregional risk sharing through public insurance as well as investment in disaster prevention, recovery, and reconstruction. The results show that public insurance encourages investment in disaster prevention, recovery, and reconstruction. Using the Great East Japan Earthquake as a case study, we conduct a computable general equilibrium analysis to quantitatively demonstrate the asymmetric spillover effects of the earthquake and reconstruction investment, and clarify the extent to which public insurance improves welfare.

Keywords Risk sharing · Spillover effect · Computable general equilibrium

---

N. Sakamoto (✉)
Faculty of Humanities and Social Sciences, Yamagata University, Yamagata, Japan
e-mail: nsakamoto@human.kj.yamagata-u.ac.jp

K. Nakajima
School of Human Science and Environment, University of Hyogo, Hyogo, Japan
e-mail: nakajima@shse.u-hyogo.ac.jp

K. N. Hirono, K. Yaguchi (eds.), *Reconstruction Period and the Stages of Regeneration After a Great Earthquake*, New Frontiers in Regional Science: Asian Perspectives 83, https://doi.org/10.1007/978-981-96-8822-7_6

6.1 Introduction

On March 11, 2011, Japan was struck by the Great East Japan Earthquake, the most powerful earthquake to hit the country in recorded history. Recovery and reconstruction plans required vast amounts of money and time, and there was much debate on the sources of revenue to fund these efforts. The earthquake shared key characteristics with other natural disasters that have occurred worldwide. Assuming that all residents should be compensated for damage impartially, a system that serves this function, if it exists, would strengthen the sense of security from the effects of natural disasters. In particular, it is important for countries that face frequent natural disasters, such as Japan, to develop a security system related to natural disasters. Such a system not only would avoid disputes over who pays how much for natural disasters, it would also prevent the spread of damage and accelerate recovery. This chapter focuses on a decentralized interregional risk-sharing system for national disasters through public insurance, as well as investment in disaster prevention, recovery, and reconstruction.

Large-scale public projects with long-term effects, such as recovery and reconstruction from natural disasters, can be financed through public bonds. However, in a country such as Japan, which has huge government debt, it would be difficult to implement such financing in a fiscally sustainable way. In addition, public bond financing can reduce private investment and consumption by future generations. Therefore, public bonds alone might not be sufficient to finance recovery from natural disasters given the sustainability of public finances and the burden on future generations. Once a major disaster occurs, financial instability and negative macroeconomic effects can arise if public debt is used to finance recovery and reconstruction.

Furthermore, even the effects of a large-scale natural disaster are not uniform across a country, weakening with distance from the affected area. For example, the Great East Japan Earthquake directly impacted the Tohoku region and its surrounds, but its effects reached the rest of the country indirectly because of, for example, disrupted supply chains and reduced tourism opportunities in those areas. Hence, natural disaster rehabilitation and reconstruction projects are considered to have asymmetric spillover effects on a disaster-stricken area (DSA) and the rest of the country.

Persson and Tabellini (1996a, b) discussed a decentralized interregional risk-sharing system for national disasters by constructing a model with two regions and an immobile population. Mansoorian (2000) extended their model to an imperfect mobile population based on Myers (1990) and Mansoorian and Myers (1993). These studies use a principal–agent model between national and regional authorities. Ihori (1999) specified interregional risk sharing using a two-person or two-region economy model with pure public goods, where the risk of income decreases for each person, and showed that perfect welfare equalization between individuals is realized by using mutual insurance and public goods provision simultaneously, irrespective of differences in income between individuals. This result is based on the neutrality theorem for private provision of public goods proposed by Shibata (1971), Warr (1983), and Ihori (1992).

In this chapter, we develop an economic model in which income loss due to a natural disaster is asymmetrically distributed across regions and investment in disaster prevention, recovery, and reconstruction reduces income loss or increases income after the disaster. In addition, we theoretically investigate optimal interregional risk sharing through a fiscal system of public insurance and investment in disaster prevention, recovery, and reconstruction. Ihori (1999) used an economic model in which the decrease in regional or individual income due to natural disasters is heterogeneous but exogenous. We endogenize the decrease in regional income through investment in disaster prevention, recovery, and reconstruction. Furthermore, while interregional risk sharing is an ex ante policy in our theoretical analysis, we conduct a quantitative analysis of the ex post policy using the Great East Japan Earthquake as a case study. Specifically, we develop a spatial computable general equilibrium (SCGE) model for Japan to measure the damage caused by the Great East Japan Earthquake and the effects of reconstruction investment and public insurance on social welfare, real GDP, and production output. We show that natural disasters and reconstruction investment have asymmetric spillover effects on income and discuss the policy implications of both reconstruction investment and public insurance.

The remainder of this chapter is organized as follows. Section 6.2 presents the economic model with asymmetric income spillovers across regions. After analyzing the effects of public insurance and investment in disaster prevention, recovery, and reconstruction as interregional risk-sharing policy instruments, we identify the conditions for the social optimum. Furthermore, we show that it is possible to realize the social optimum as a decentralized Nash equilibrium under a certain fiscal system and highlight the role of public insurance. Section 6.3 presents our SCGE model consisting of 47 prefectures and 20 industrial sectors in Japan to analyze the impact of the Great East Japan Earthquake and the effect of reconstruction investment and public insurance. We measure the change in social welfare (ex post utility), real GDP, and production output across prefectures due to the earthquake to show its asymmetric spillover effect on regional income, assuming that the earthquake caused private capital stock in the DSA to collapse. Furthermore, we show the effects of public insurance and the asymmetric spillover effects of reconstruction investment on regional income across prefectures. Section 6.4 presents conclusions and future research topics.

6.2 Theoretical Model

We develop a simple two-region model with asymmetric spillover effects of natural disasters and policy instruments on regional income. The model is assumed to simultaneously include disaster-prevention investment, recovery and reconstruction investment, and public insurance as policy instruments for interregional risk sharing. In this section, we analyze their effects from a normative perspective.

6.2.1 An Economic Model with Asymmetric Spillover Effect

The economy consists of regions 1 and 2, facing states A and B. State A denotes a state with a natural disaster and occurs with probability α. State B denotes a state without a natural disaster and occurs with probability $1 - \alpha$. When a natural disaster occurs, only region 1 is affected. In this case, income of region 1 is assumed to decrease, whereas that of region 2 may increase or decrease. Next, we consider interregional risk-sharing instruments. We assume that investments in disaster prevention are made before the state is determined; that is, before the natural disaster occurs, the effects are realized only when the disaster occurs. Investments in recovery and reconstruction are made only after a natural disaster has occurred and their effects are realized only when the natural disaster occurs. Investments in disaster prevention are costly regardless of whether a natural disaster occurs; however, investments in recovery and reconstruction are costly only when a natural disaster occurs.

In state A, region i has exogenous income Y_i. In state B, region i has endogenous income $f^i(P, R)$, where P is disaster-prevention investment and R is recovery and reconstruction investment. Both types of investment can be made only for region 1. If neither investment type is made, then region 1 in state B has a lower income than in state A. If either type is made, then the income of region 1 in state B increases. Meanwhile, the income of region 2 increases or decreases owing to the natural disaster or investments, because production disruptions in region 1 increase the production of region 2, or investments increase the fiscal burden in region 2. Therefore, we assume for region 1 only:

$$f^1(0,0) - Y_1 < 0, \tag{6.1}$$

$$f_P^1(P,R) > 0, \tag{6.2}$$

$$f_R^1(P,R) > 0. \tag{6.3}$$

If $f^1(0, 0) - Y_1 = f^2(0, 0) - Y_2$, then the effects of a natural disaster on regions 1 and 2 are symmetric if no investment is made in disaster prevention, recovery, and reconstruction. Similarly, if $f_P^1(P,R) = f_P^2(P,R)$ and $f_R^1(P,R) = f_R^2(P,R)$, then the effects of investments in disaster prevention, recovery, and reconstruction for regions 1 and 2 are symmetric when a natural disaster occurs. However, we assume that the effects of natural disasters and investments in regions 1 and region 2 are not symmetric. In the economy as a whole, total income is assumed to be reduced by the natural disaster and increased by investments; that is,

$$f^1(0,0) + f^2(0,0) - Y_1 - Y_2 < 0, \tag{6.4}$$

$$f_P^1(P,R)+f_P^2(P,R)>0, \tag{6.5}$$

$$f_R^1(P,R)+f_R^2(P,R)>0. \tag{6.6}$$

These assumptions imply that natural disasters are harmful but that investments to mitigate them are beneficial to the entire economy.

6.2.2 Social Optimum

We assume that each region's utility function depends only on private consumption, which is state-dependent. The expected utility function of region i is

$$W_i=(1-\alpha)V\left(c_i^A\right)+\alpha V\left(c_i^B\right), \tag{6.7}$$

where c_i^A and c_i^B are the consumption of private goods in region i in states A and B, respectively. We assume that $V' > 0$ and $V'' < 0$.The social planner is constrained by the feasibility restrictions for the entire economy in each state:

$$Y_1+Y_2-c_1^A-c_2^A-P=0, \tag{6.8}$$

$$f^1(P,R)+f^2(P,R)-c_1^B-c_2^B-P-R=0, \tag{6.9}$$

where the marginal rate of transformation between private goods and investments is assumed to be unity.

Efficient allocations can be characterized by maximizing the linear combination of W_1 and W_2 under feasibility restrictions. Therefore, the efficient allocations solve the following problem for all $\delta \in [0, 1]$:

$$\max_{c_1^A,c_2^A,c_1^B,c_2^B,P,R} \delta\left\{(1-\alpha)V\left(c_1^A\right)+\alpha V\left(c_1^B\right)\right\}+(1-\delta)\left\{(1-\alpha)V\left(c_2^A\right)+\alpha V\left(c_2^B\right)\right\}$$

$$\text{subject to Eqs.}(6.8)\text{and}(6.9) \tag{6.10}$$

λ^A and λ^B denote the Lagrange multipliers associated with the feasibility restrictions in states A and B, respectively; then, first-order conditions are

$$\delta(1-\alpha)V'\left(c_1^A\right)-\lambda^A=0, \tag{6.11}$$

$$(1-\delta)(1-\alpha)V'\left(c_2^A\right)-\lambda^A=0, \tag{6.12}$$

$$\delta\alpha V'\left(c_1^B\right)-\lambda^B=0, \tag{6.13}$$

$$(1-\delta)\alpha V'\left(c_2^B\right)-\lambda^B=0, \tag{6.14}$$

$$-\lambda^A+\lambda^B\left\{f_P^1(P,R)+f_P^2(P,R)-1\right\}=0, \tag{6.15}$$

$$\lambda^B\left\{f_R^1(P,R)+f_R^2(P,R)-1\right\}=0. \tag{6.16}$$

Eliminating λ^A in Eqs. (6.11) and (6.12) and λ^B in Eqs. (6.13) and (6.14) yields

$$\delta V'\left(c_1^A\right)=(1-\delta)V'\left(c_2^A\right), \tag{6.17}$$

$$\delta V'\left(c_1^B\right)=(1-\delta)V'\left(c_2^B\right). \tag{6.18}$$

Moreover, eliminating δ in Eqs. (6.17) and (6.18), we obtain

$$\frac{V'\left(c_1^A\right)}{V'\left(c_1^B\right)}=\frac{V'\left(c_2^A\right)}{V'\left(c_2^B\right)}. \tag{6.19}$$

Equation (6.19) shows that the marginal rates of substitution between consumptions in states A and B are equal across regions in the social optimum, regardless of welfare weight δ.

Inserting Eqs. (6.11), (6.13) into (6.15) yields

$$f_P^1(P,R)+f_P^2(P,R)=1+\frac{1-\alpha}{\alpha}\frac{V'\left(c_i^A\right)}{V'\left(c_i^B\right)}. \tag{6.20}$$

Equation (6.20) can be considered the Samuelson rule for investment in disaster prevention. The left-hand side represents the marginal benefit and the right-hand side represents the marginal cost. The first term on the right-hand side is the marginal rate of transformation, and the second term is the consumption sacrificed by disaster-prevention investment in state A, measured in monetary terms in state B.

Finally, we induce the Samuelson rule for investment in recovery and reconstruction from Eq. (6.16):

$$f_R^1(P,R)+f_R^2(P,R)=1. \tag{6.21}$$

Will Nash-competing regions accept the socially optimal allocation characterized by Eqs. (6.19), (6.20), and (6.21)? After examining the exogenous effects of policy instruments for risk sharing on expected utility, we will consider this problem.

6.2.3 Risk-Sharing Instruments

Next, we introduce public insurance as a policy instrument for risk sharing, in addition to investments in disaster prevention, recovery, and reconstruction, and analyze their effects on the expected utility of each region. The central government invests P in disaster prevention and R in recovery and reconstruction. Region i's shares of these costs are θ_i^P and θ_i^R, respectively. In addition, region i is covered by public insurance with return S_i and price p. The feasibility restrictions for region 1 in each state are as follows.

$$Y_i - c_i^A - \theta_i^P P - pS_i = 0, \tag{6.22}$$

$$f^i(P, R) - c_i^B - \theta_i^P P - \theta_i^R R - pS_i + S_i = 0. \tag{6.23}$$

Substituting Eqs. (6.22) and (6.23) solved for c_i^A and c_i^B into (6.7), partially differentiating by P, R, and S_i and evaluating at $P = 0$, $R = 0$, and $S_i = 0$, respectively, we obtain

$$\left.\frac{\partial W_i}{\partial P}\right|_{P=0} = -\theta_i^P(1-\alpha)V'(Y_i - pS_i) + \alpha V'\left(f^i(0, R) - \theta_i^R R + (1-p)S_i\right) \left(f_P^i(0, R) - \theta_i^P\right), \tag{6.24}$$

$$\left.\frac{\partial W_i}{\partial R}\right|_{R=0} = \alpha V'\left(f^i(P, 0) - \theta_i^P P + (1-p)S_i\right)\left(f_R^i(P, 0) - \theta_i^R\right), \tag{6.25}$$

$$\left.\frac{\partial W_i}{\partial S_i}\right|_{S_i=0} = -p(1-\alpha)V'\left(Y_i - \theta_i^P P\right) + (1-p)\alpha V'\left(f^i(P, R) - \theta_i^P P - \theta_i^R R\right), \tag{6.26}$$

Equation (6.24) shows that if θ_1^P is zero or sufficiently low, disaster-prevention investment increases the expected utility of region 1, the DSA. Even if θ_1^P is somewhat high, if the effect of disaster reduction investment on region 1 is large, the expected utility of region 1 increases. Therefore, for investment in disaster prevention to increase the expected utility of the DSA, it is necessary to set the cost burden lower than the investment effect in the DSA. Furthermore, Eq. (6.24) implies that if $f_P^2(0,R)$ is zero or negative, disaster-prevention investment decreases the expected utility of region 2, the non-DSA. Thus, for investment in disaster prevention to increase the expected utility of region 2, disaster-prevention investments must increase the income in region 2.

The discussion above for Eq. (6.24) also applies to Eq. (6.25). In region 1, if the effect of recovery and reconstruction investment on income is greater than the cost burden, the expected utility is increased by that investment. In region 2, for the expected utility to increase owing to the recovery and reconstruction investment, income must also increase by that investment. Therefore, it is difficult for all regions to agree on the cost burden of disaster-prevention, recovery, and reconstruction investments, because these investments may reduce income in non-DSA.

The central government is assumed to provide public insurance to all regions. Assuming a fair price, where insurance revenue equals insurance payment, that is, $p = \alpha$, from Eq. (6.26), we obtain the following equation by $V'' < 0$.

$$sgn\left(\left.\frac{\partial W_i}{\partial S_i}\right|_{S_i=0}\right) = sgn\left(Y_i - f^i\left(P, R\right) + \theta_i^R R\right). \tag{6.27}$$

Under a given investment in disaster prevention, recovery, and reconstruction, the expected utility of each region always increases by public insurance if income is reduced because of natural disasters. Even if income increases because of natural disasters, the expected utility increases if the burden of investment in recovery and reconstruction is greater than the increase in income. This implies that with public insurance, the cost of investment in recovery and reconstruction can be covered by the burden on regions where income increases because of natural disasters.

6.2.4 Decentralized Nash Equilibrium

We analyze a decentralized policy decision on public insurance, disaster-prevention, and recovery and reconstruction investments. P and R consist of the contributions or voluntary tax burdens from each region,

$$P = g_1^P + g_2^P, \tag{6.28}$$

$$R = g_1^R + g_2^R, \tag{6.29}$$

where g_i^P and g_i^R denote region i's contributions to P and R, respectively.

The feasibility restrictions of region i in each state are

$$c_i^A = Y_i - \left(1 - \beta_i^P\right) g_i^P - pS_i, \tag{6.30}$$

$$c_i^B = f^i\left(P, R\right) - \left(1 - \beta_i^P\right) g_i^P - \left(1 - \beta_i^P\right) g_i^R - pS_i + S_i, \tag{6.31}$$

where β_i^P and β_i^R are subsidy rates for disaster-prevention, and recovery and reconstruction investments, respectively. By eliminating g_i^P, g_i^R, and S_i in Eqs. (6.28), (6.29), (6.30), and (6.31), we obtain the integrated feasibility restriction for region i:

$$(1-p)Y_i + pf^i\left(P,R\right) + \left(1 - \beta_i^P\right) g_j^P + p\left(1 - \beta_i^R\right) g_j^R - (1-p)c_i^A - pc_i^B - \left(1 - \beta_i^P\right) P - p\left(1 - \beta_i^R\right) R = 0 \tag{6.32}$$

Given g_j^P and g_j^R, the local government in region i solves the following problem:

$$\max_{c_i^A, c_i^B, P, R} (1-\alpha)V\left(c_i^A\right)+\alpha V\left(c_i^B\right),$$

$$\text{subject to Eq.}(6.32). \tag{6.33}$$

Assuming the existence of an interior solution for c_i^A and c_i^B, the first-order conditions for $i = 1, 2$, are

$$(1-\alpha)V'\left(c_i^A\right)-(1-p)\lambda_i=0, \tag{6.34}$$

$$\alpha V'\left(c_i^B\right)-p\lambda_i=0, \tag{6.35}$$

$$\lambda_i\left\{pf_P^i(P,R)-\left(1-\beta_i^P\right)\right\}\leq 0, P\geq 0, \text{and } P\lambda_i\left\{pf_P^i(P,R)-\left(1-\beta_i^P\right)\right\}=0, \tag{6.36}$$

$$\lambda_i p\left\{f_R^i(P,R)-\left(1-\beta_i^R\right)\right\}\leq 0, R\geq 0, \text{and } R\lambda_i p\left\{f_R^i(P,R)-\left(1-\beta_i^R\right)\right\}=0, \tag{6.37}$$

where λ_i is the Lagrange multiplier for Eq. (6.32). Eliminating λ_i in (6.34) and (6.35), we obtain

$$\frac{1-\alpha}{\alpha}\frac{V'\left(c_i^A\right)}{V'\left(c_i^B\right)}=\frac{1-p}{p}. \tag{6.38}$$

Because α and p are common to both regions, it follows that Eq. (6.19), which is a necessary condition for the social optimum, can be obtained from Eq. (6.38). Moreover, if disaster-prevention as well as recovery and reconstruction investments are positive in Nash equilibrium, then

$$pf_P^i(P,R)=1-\beta_i^P, \tag{6.39}$$

$$f_R^i(P,R)=1-\beta_i^R, \tag{6.40}$$

should be satisfied for $i = 1, 2$. Thus, for these investments to be positive, the central government should set β_i^P and β_i^R to be less than 1 for the region where $f_P^i(P,R)>0$ and $f_R^i(P,R)>0$ but greater than 1 for the region where $f_P^i(P,R)<0$ and $f_R^i(P,R)<0$. Consequently, if investments in disaster prevention as well as recovery and reconstruction have negative spillover effects on a non-DSA, the central government should set a subsidy rate greater than 1 for the voluntary tax burden of the area to motivate the area to accept positive investments. Such a subsidy plays a role in internalizing negative external effects in non-DSA.

Furthermore, summing Eqs. (6.39) and (6.40) with respect to i yields

$$pf_P^1(P,R)+pf_P^2(P,R)=2-\beta_1^P-\beta_2^P, \tag{6.41}$$

$$f_R^1(P,R)+f_R^2(P,R)=2-\beta_1^R-\beta_2^R. \tag{6.42}$$

If we assume the fair price $p = \alpha$, then, from Eq. (6.38),

$$c_i^A = c_i^B, \tag{6.43}$$

should hold for $i = 1, 2$. In addition, if $\beta_1^P + \beta_2^P = 1$, then we can induce Eq. (6.20) from (6.41) and (6.43). Similarly, if $\beta_1^R + \beta_2^R = 1$ holds, Eq. (6.21) can be obtained from (6.42).

Based on this normative analysis, we conclude that if $p = \alpha$, $\beta_1^P + \beta_2^P = 1$, and $\beta_1^R + \beta_2^R = 1$, then an interior Nash equilibrium across regions is socially optimal. This is compatible with the incentives for each region under the above conditions. We examine the structure of subsidies that realize positive investments in the Nash equilibrium in more detail. If investments in disaster prevention, and recovery and reconstruction for region 1, that is, the DSA, have a positive spillover effect on region 2, that is, the non-DSA, then $0 < 1 - \beta_1^P = \beta_2^P < 1$ and $0 < 1 - \beta_1^R = \beta_2^R < 1$ should hold. Therefore, the central government is required to set a subsidy rate higher than 0% and lower than 100% for both regions to achieve the social optimum. In the efficient allocation of resources, regions 1 and 2 have a lower tax burden because they receive Pigouvian subsidies from each other that internalize the positive externalities of these investments. Meanwhile, if these investments have a negative spillover effect on region 2, then $1 < \beta_2^P = 1 - \beta_1^P$ and $1 < \beta_2^R = 1 - \beta_1^R$ should hold. Thus, the central government must set a subsidy rate that is negative for region 1 and another subsidy rate that is greater than 100% for region 2. Thus, region 1 bears a heavier tax burden because, in addition to its voluntary tax burden, it must bear a Pigouvian tax to internalize the negative external effects of these investments in region 2. Region 2 also has an overall negative tax burden, that is, receives a subsidy, because it receives a Pigouvian subsidy to offset both the negative external effects of these investments on its own region and to internalize the positive external effects of these investments in region 1. If these investments have negative spillover effects on region 2, especially ex post, the tax burden on region 1 is high, but public insurance reduces the ex post tax burden and consumption is equalized across states as shown in Eq. (7.43). Thus, the effective burden on region 1 is not higher ex post than ex ante.

6.2.5 The Role of Public Insurance

Public insurance not only equalizes consumption across states in each region, but also ensures optimal investments in disaster prevention. Moreover, if investments in disaster prevention encourage investments in recovery and reconstruction, public insurance complement to investments in recovery and reconstruction as well as disaster prevention.

Assuming $S_i = 0$, Eqs. (6.30) and (6.31) are rewritten as

$$c_i^A = Y_i - \left(1 - \beta_i^P\right) g_i^P, \tag{6.44}$$

$$c_i^B = f^i(P,R) - (1-\beta_i^P)g_i^P - (1-\beta_i^P)g_i^R = f^i(P,R) + c_i^A - Y_i - (1-\beta_i^R)g_i^R. \quad (6.45)$$

By eliminating g_i^P and g_i^R in Eqs. (6.44) and (6.45) and using (6.28) and (6.29), we obtain

$$Y_i + (1-\beta_i^P)g_j^P - c_i^A - (1-\beta_i^P)P = 0, \quad (6.46)$$

$$c_i^B = c_i^A - Y_i + f^i(P,R) + (1-\beta_i^R)g_j^R - (1-\beta_i^R)R \quad (6.47)$$

Given g_j^P and g_j^R, the local government in region i solves the following problem:

$$\max_{c_i^A,P,R} (1-\alpha)V(c_i^A) + \alpha V\left(c_i^A - Y_i + f^i(P,R) + (1-\beta_i^R)g_j^R - (1-\beta_i^R)R\right),$$

$$\text{subject to Eq.}(6.46). \quad (6.48)$$

Assuming the existence of an interior solution for c_i^A and c_i^B, the first-order conditions for $i = 1, 2$, are

$$(1-\alpha)V'(c_i^A) + \alpha V'(c_i^B) - \mu_i = 0, \quad (6.49)$$

$$\alpha V'(c_i^B) f_P^i(P,R) - \mu_i(1-\beta_i^P) \le 0, P \ge 0,$$

$$P\{\alpha V'(c_i^B) f_P^i(P,R) - \mu_i(1-\beta_i^P)\} = 0, \quad (6.50)$$

$$\alpha V'(c_i^B)\{f_R^i(P,R) - (1-\beta_i^R)\} \le 0, R \ge 0, R\alpha V'(c_i^B)$$
$$\{f_R^i(P,R) - (1-\beta_i^R)\} = 0. \quad (6.51)$$

where μ_i is the Lagrange multiplier for Eq. (7.32). If investments in disaster prevention are positive in a Nash equilibrium, Eqs. (6.49) and (6.50) can be rewritten by eliminating μ_i as follows:

$$f_P^i(P,R) = \left(1 + \frac{1-\alpha}{\alpha}\frac{V'(c_i^A)}{V'(c_i^B)}\right)(1-\beta_i^P). \quad (6.52)$$

Furthermore, summing up (7.52) with respect to i yields

$$f_P^1(P,R) + f_P^2(P,R) = \left(1 + \frac{1-\alpha}{\alpha}\frac{V'(c_1^A)}{V'(c_1^B)}\right)(1-\beta_1^P)$$
$$+ \left(1 + \frac{1-\alpha}{\alpha}\frac{V'(c_2^A)}{V'(c_2^B)}\right)(1-\beta_2^P). \quad (6.53)$$

Equation (6.53) does not coincide with Eq. (7.20) even if $\beta_1^P + \beta_2^P = 1$ holds. Therefore, the Nash equilibrium without public insurance is not socially optimal. If public insurance exists, then Eq. (6.20) is induced from Eq. (6.53), because Eq. (6.43) hold. This implies that public insurance complement investments in disaster prevention. Moreover, in Eq. (6.51), the non-optimality of investments in disaster prevention may prevent the realization of positive investments in recovery and reconstruction. In this case, public insurance complement investments in recovery and reconstruction. If we have positive investments in recovery and reconstruction under $\beta_1^R + \beta_2^R = 1$, then these investments are socially optimal.

6.3 Numerical Analysis

In the theoretical model, we assume that not only natural disasters but also investments in disaster prevention as well as recovery and reconstruction have asymmetric spillover effects on income ex post and analyze their effects on expected utility across regions and the fiscal system for risk sharing. In this section, we use an SCGE model to quantitatively investigate the existence of asymmetric spillover effects of the Great East Japan Earthquake. Specifically, we show how the earthquake caused asymmetric changes in production output, real GDP, and social welfare in each prefecture owing to the loss of private capital stock and investment in recovery and reconstruction. We also show how reconstruction investment and income compensation through public insurance change production output, real GDP, and social welfare in each prefecture.

6.3.1 Structure of Spatial Computable General Equilibrium Model

This study develops an SCGE model that consists of 47 prefectures and 20 industrial sectors in Japan using the 2000 Interregional Input-Output table developed by Miyagi et al. (2003) and Ishikawa and Miyagi (2004) as the reference data set. As shown in Tables 6.1 and 6.2, we integrate 45 production sectors into 20 production sectors, covering 47 prefectures in Japan. For population data in each prefecture, we use the 2000 population census of Japan by the Ministry of Internal Affairs and Communication (2001) (see Tables 6.1 and 6.2). In the following, we assume that $S(s \in S)$ is the set of regions (47 prefectures) that goods are consumed, $R(r \in R)$ is the set of regions (47 prefectures) that goods are produced, $I(i \in I)$ is the set of goods, and $J(j \in J)$ is the set of 20 production sectors. In addition, we use the Armington (1969) assumption, whereby goods domestically produced or consumed and those imported or exported are imperfectly substitutable with each other (Hosoe et al. 2010).

Table 6.1 Production sector classification in SCGE model

No.	20 sectors in SCGE	Code	45 production sectors in 47 prefectural IO table
1	Agriculture	AGR	Agriculture
2	Forestry	FRS	Forestry
3	Fishery	FSH	Fishery
4	Mining	MIN	Mining
5	Foods	FOD	Foods
6	Other manufacturing	OMF	Textile products, Timber & wooden products, Furniture & fixtures, Pulp, paper, paperboard & building paper, Publishing & Printing, Leather, fur skins & miscellaneous leather products, Ceramic, stone & clay products, Miscellaneous manufacturing products
7	Chemical products	CPR	Chemical products, Plastic products, Rubber products
8	Petroleum and coal products	P_C	Petroleum & coal products
9	Iron and steel	I_S	Iron & steel
10	Metal products	MTL	Non-ferrous metals, Metal products
11	Machinery	MCH	General industrial machinery, Machinery for office & service industry, Motor Vehicles, Other transportation equipment
12	Electronic equipment	ELM	Household electronic & electric appliances, Electronic & communication equipment, Other electrical equipment, Precision instruments
13	Construction	CNS	Building construction & repair of construction, Public construction & other civil engineering
14	Electricity	ELY	Electricity
15	Gas and heat supply	GDT	Gas & heat supply
16	Water supply	WTR	Water supply & waste management services
17	Commerce	COM	Wholesale & retail trade, Finance & insurance, Real estate
18	Transport	TRS	Transport
19	Medical services	MED	Medical service, health and social security & nursing care
20	Other services	ANC	Communication & broadcasting, Education & research, Public administration, Other public services, Business services, Personal services, Activities not elsewhere classified

Table 6.2 Regional classification in SCGE model

No.	Pref.	Code	No.	Pref.	Code	No.	Pref.	Code
1	Hokkaido	HKD	17	Ishikawa	ISK	33	Okayama	OKY
2	Aomori	AMR	18	Fukui	FKI	34	Hiroshima	HRS
3	Iwate	IWT	19	Yamanashi	YMN	35	Yamaguchi	YGC
4	Miyagi	MYG	20	Nagano	NGN	36	Tokushima	TKS
5	Akita	AKT	21	Gifu	GIF	37	Kagawa	KGW
6	Yamagata	YGT	22	Shizuoka	SZK	38	Ehime	EHM
7	Fukushima	FKS	23	Aichi	ACH	39	Kochi	KOC
8	Ibaraki	IBR	24	Mie	MIE	40	Fukuoka	FKO
9	Tochigi	TCG	25	Shiga	SIG	41	Saga	SAG
10	Gunma	GMM	26	Kyoto	KYT	42	Nagasaki	NGS
11	Saitama	STM	27	Osaka	OSK	43	Kumamoto	KMT
12	Chiba	CHB	28	Hyogo	HYG	44	Oita	OIT
13	Tokyo	TKY	29	Nara	NAR	45	Miyazaki	MYZ
14	Kanagawa	KNG	30	Wakayama	WKY	46	Kagoshima	KGS
15	Niigata	NGT	31	Tottori	TTR	47	Okinawa	OKW
16	Toyama	TYM	32	Shimane	SMN			

Production Sector

As shown in Fig. 6.1a, all production functions in the domestic production sector are assumed to follow a nested CES (constant elasticity of substitution) style (see Fig. 6.1a). In the first step, labor L_j^s and capital K_j^s are aggregated into a composite production factor VA_j^s using a Cobb–Douglas production function, and the composite inputs N_{ij}^s are composed of intermediate inputs X_{ij}^{rs} from all regions using a CES production function.

In the second step, to produce gross domestic output Y_j^s for the *j*th production sector in the *s*th region, the composite production factor is combined with composite inputs, using a Leontief production function.

Household Sector

Figure 6.1b shows the household consumption structure (see Fig. 6.1b). We assume that there is one representative household in each region. To yield utility U_H^s under a budget constraint, a household demands composite household consumption goods N_{iH}^s composed of intermediate household consumption X_{iH}^{rs} from all regions using a CES function.

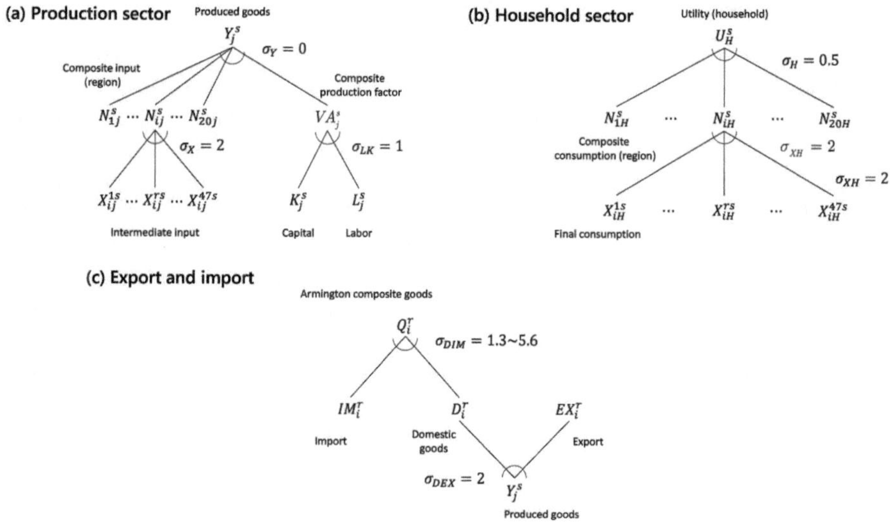

Fig. 6.1 Structure of (**a**) production sector, (**b**) household sector, and (**c**) export and import sector

Government Sector

Based on Ban (2007), we assume that there is no central government that collects national taxes, provides national public goods, or redistributes income, but that the government sector in each region divides its expenditure into government consumption and government investment. However, this assumption is made only in the model; we assume that reconstruction investment and public insurance are carried out implicitly by the central government. The government sector in each region earns revenue from income tax, production tax, and indirect tax and, under budget constraints, determines optimal consumption and investment. In addition, the government sector in each region is assumed to be myopic about investment and demands investment goods in its own region.

Private and Government Investment Sector

As Fig. 6.1b shows, the structure of private and government investments is assumed to be the same as that of household consumption. We also assume that there is one virtual private and one government investment agent in each region. Total savings for total investments consist of the sum of household savings, government savings, foreign savings, and income transfers in each region. While the government sector invests in its own region, the private investment sector demands investment in goods across the region. Table 6.3 shows the proportions of private and public capital formation in the 47 prefectures (see Table 6.3).

Table 6.3 Proportion of private and public capital formation in 47 prefectures

	Private	Public		Private	Public		Private	Public
Hokkaido	0.517	0.483	Ishikawa	0.653	0.347	Okayama	0.673	0.327
Aomori	0.644	0.356	Fukui	0.623	0.377	Hiroshima	0.722	0.278
Iwate	0.570	0.430	Yamanashi	0.669	0.331	Yamaguchi	0.669	0.331
Miyagi	0.715	0.285	Nagano	0.673	0.327	Tokushima	0.625	0.375
Akita	0.564	0.436	Gifu	0.642	0.358	Kagawa	0.745	0.255
Yamagata	0.655	0.345	Shizuoka	0.791	0.209	Ehime	0.668	0.332
Fukushima	0.719	0.281	Aichi	0.823	0.177	Kochi	0.507	0.493
Ibaraki	0.718	0.282	Mie	0.758	0.242	Fukuoka	0.715	0.285
Tochigi	0.765	0.235	Shiga	0.736	0.264	Saga	0.622	0.378
Gunma	0.749	0.251	Kyoto	0.694	0.306	Nagasaki	0.611	0.389
Saitama	0.788	0.212	Osaka	0.816	0.184	Kumamoto	0.677	0.323
Chiba	0.749	0.251	Hyogo	0.721	0.279	Oita	0.693	0.307
Tokyo	0.837	0.163	Nara	0.622	0.378	Miyazaki	0.587	0.413
Kanagawa	0.802	0.198	Wakayama	0.567	0.433	Kagoshima	0.577	0.423
Niigata	0.645	0.355	Tottori	0.579	0.421	Okinawa	0.567	0.433
Toyama	0.683	0.317	Shimane	0.462	0.538			

Exports and Imports

In accordance with Hosoe et al. (2010), Fig. 6.1c shows the structure of substitution between imports and domestic goods and that of the transformation between exports and domestic goods (see Fig. 6.1c). Regarding imperfect substitution between imports and domestic goods, we adopt the Armington's assumption. The ith Armington-composite-good-producing sector in the sth region aggregates domestic goods D_i^r and imports IM_i^r into composite goods Q_i^r using a CES function. Meanwhile, gross domestic output Y_i^r is transformed into domestic goods D_i^r and exports EX_i^r using a CET (constant elasticity of transformation) function. While the parameters of elasticity of transformation σ_{DEX} are assumed to be 2.0 exogenously, the parameters of elasticity of substitution σ_{DIM} are set to the values estimated by GTAP7.1, as shown in Table 6.4.

Market Clearance Condition

To meet the demand and supply in all markets, market equilibrium conditions are imposed in Eqs. (6.54) to (6.57), respectively.

$$Q_i^r = \Sigma_s \Sigma_j X_{ij}^{rs} + \Sigma_s X_{iH}^{rs} + \Sigma_s X_{iG}^{rs} + \Sigma_s XI_{iH}^{rs} + \Sigma_s XI_{iG}^{rs}, \tag{6.54}$$

$$\overline{L^s} = \Sigma_j L_j^s, \tag{6.55}$$

Table 6.4 Setting values of elasticity of substitution

Production sector	Value	Production sector	Value
Agriculture	2.5	Machinery	3.6
Forestry	2.5	Electronic equipment	4.4
Fishery	1.3	Construction	1.9
Mining	5.6	Electricity	2.8
Foods	2.5	Gas and heat supply	2.8
Other manufacturing	3.4	Water supply	2.8
Chemical products	3.3	Commerce	1.9
Petroleum and coal products	2.1	Transport	1.9
Iron and steel	3.0	Medical services	1.9
Metal products	3.9	Other services	1.9

$$\overline{K^s} = \sum_j K_j^s, \tag{6.56}$$

$$\sum_s TR^s = 0, \tag{6.57}$$

where X_{iG}^{rs} is the government consumption, XI_{iH}^{rs} is the private investment, and XI_{iG}^{rs} is the government investment. Equation (6.54) shows the market equilibrium conditions for Armington goods, which means that its supply meets the sum of the demand for intermediate input goods, household consumption goods, government consumption goods, private investment goods, and government investment goods. Equation (6.55) is the equilibrium condition for the labor market and Eq. (6.56) for capital markets. Then, Eq. (6.57) indicates that the sum of income transfer in all regions is zero.

6.3.2 Setting of Scenarios for the Great East Japan Earthquake and Reconstruction Strategies

In this study, the Tohoku region, which includes Iwate, Miyagi, Fukushima, and Ibaraki, is assumed as the DSA due to the Great East Japan Earthquake. The direct impacts of the earthquake on DSA were assumed to spill over to economic activities in areas that included 20 production sectors in 47 prefectures. In addition, assuming that both capital stock and labor in the DSA were damaged simultaneously to make the model and interpret the results more complex, we focus only on capital stock damage in the DSA. To measure the economic impact of capital stock damage and the effects of reconstruction investment and public insurance on the DSA, we set the following three scenarios:

1. Supply constraint by collapsed private capital stock in the DSA.
2. Regional redistribution by reconstruction investment in the DSA.
3. Income compensation by public insurance in the DSA.

In addition, in our simulation analysis of reconstruction investment and public insurance, by comparing scenarios with private capital stock damaged and with reconstruction investment or public insurance, the differences between two scenarios are considered as the effects of reconstruction investment or public insurance. In the results below, note that if the change in an economic index is positive, then the economic condition can be improved through reconstruction investment or public insurance. However, if the change is negative, it can worsen.

1. ***Supply Constraint Scenario***

   After the Great East Japan Earthquake in 2011, the Cabinet Office, Government of Japan (2011a, b), and the Development Bank of Japan (2011a, b) estimated direct damage to capital stock, as shown in Table 6.5. As for the seven prefectures, Hokkaido, Aomori, Iwate, Miyagi, Fukushima, Ibaraki, and Chiba, the Cabinet Office, Government of Japan (2011a, b) estimated damage from about 16 trillion yen to about 25 trillion yen. Similarly, the Development Bank of Japan (2011a, b) estimated the damage to be approximately 16 trillion yen. From this estimation, it is likely that the sum of capital stock damage in Iwate, Miyagi, Fukushima, and Ibaraki was approximately 16 trillion yen and that in the Tohoku region was approximately 14 trillion yen. In addition, it should be noted that various types of damage caused by the Fukushima Daiichi nuclear disaster were not included in these estimations.

   Next, we assume capital stock damage applied in the SCGE model. Capital stock damage discussed above is based on *stock* concept. Meanwhile, since the capital stock data used in the SCGE model were based on *flow* concept, capital stock damage due to the earthquake was transformed into that of the flow concept. According to Nakajima and Sakamoto (2015), we calculate the damage rate of capital stock $\hat{\delta}^s$ in the sth region by dividing the total amount of estimated capital stock damage by the total amount of capital stock estimated. Then, by using estimated damage rates of capital stock $\hat{\delta}^s$ and an initial private capital endowment before the earthquake $K^s\,|_{t=0}$, an initial private capital endowment in the sth region after the earthquake $\overline{K^s}\,|_{t=1}$ is defined in Eq. (6.5). In addition, calculating the capital stock damage discussed above means that we apply the results estimated by the Development Bank of Japan (2011a, b), and employ direct capital stock damage of 16.4 trillion yen (3.15% of GDP) owing to the Great East Japan Earthquake.

$$\left.\overline{K^s}\right|_{t=1} = \left(1-\hat{\delta}^s\right)\bullet\left.\overline{K^s}\right|_{t=0} \tag{6.58}$$

2. ***Reconstruction Investment Scenario***

   For the reconstruction investment in our SCGE model, a virtual reconstruction agency assumes that the tax for reconstruction is collected from tax revenue in each prefecture at a certain rate and distributed into government savings in the four prefectures in the DSA as funds for reconstruction investment. We also assume a uniform 0.1% tax throughout the nation, as funds for reconstruction are collected from the tax revenue in each prefecture. Because our SCGE model has

Table 6.5 Estimation of capital stock damages by the Development Bank of Japan (2011a)

DSA		Estimated capital stock (1 B. Yen)	Estimated capital stock damage (1 billion Yen)					
			Infrastructure	House	Manufacturing	Others	Total	Damage rate (%)
Iwate	Inland	26,369	457	22	64	211	754	2.9
	Coast	7449	1943	607	191	781	3522	47.3
	Total	33,818	2400	629	255	992	4276	12.6
Miyagi	Inland	31,443	856	40	148	551	1595	5.1
	Coast	23,182	2031	1446	290	1130	4897	21.1
	Total	54,625	2887	1486	438	1681	6492	11.9
Fukushima	Inland	34,314	630	7	263	370	1270	3.7
	Coast	15,941	1244	145	151	319	1859	11.7
	Total	50,254	1874	152	414	689	3129	6.2
Ibaraki	Inland	47,827	460	40	175	318	993	2.1
	Coast	21,727	766	87	355	275	1483	6.8
	Total	69,553	1226	126	530	593	2476	3.6
Total	Inland	139,952	2403	109	650	1451	4612	3.3
	Coast	68,299	5985	2285	987	2504	11,781	17.2
	Total	208,251	8387	2394	1637	3955	16,373	7.9

a total tax revenue of approximately 82 trillion yen, the funds for reconstruction in our model are assumed to be approximately 800 billion yen. Considering that funds of approximately 25 trillion yen were allocated in the Concentrated Reconstruction Period, the funds for reconstruction in this study were very small. However, because the purpose of this study is to measure the local effects of reconstruction investment, 0.1% of the funds collected from tax revenue in each prefecture are seen as a benchmark.

3. ***Public Insurance Scenario***

   In this study, we assume that, after the Great East Japan Earthquake, income reduced by the disaster is compensated for by the insurance revenue collected before the earthquake, that is, public insurance. Compensation for income from the earthquake is provided not only in the areas affected by the earthquake but also in all areas where income has decreased after the earthquake. However, because the SCGE model in this study is static, it cannot explicitly express the intertemporal behavior of economic agents before and after the earthquake, although insurance compensation after the earthquake needs to be provided by insurance payments made before the earthquake. Therefore, it should be noted that we assume that insurance to compensate for the post-disaster income decline has already been collected.

6.3.3 Results and Discussion

1. ***Supply Constraint by Collapsed Private Capital Stock***

   First, the left-hand panel of Fig. 6.2 shows that the decrease in welfare was estimated to be 1082 billion yen per year in total and 858 billion yen per year in the DSA (see Fig. 6.2). Whereas Hayashiyama et al. (2012) estimated welfare decreases of 6.71 billion yen per year in total and 6.56 billion yen per year in the DSA, Muto et al. (2012) estimated welfare decreases of about 2500 billion yen per year and about 2270 billion yen per year in the DSA. Thus, we found that the changes in welfare due to damage to private capital stock varied widely, and our estimations were consistent with their estimations. In addition, marked decreases in welfare per capita in the upper panel of Fig. 6.3 were estimated, respectively, as 145.2 thousand yen per year in Miyagi, 150.9 thousand yen per year in Iwate, and a total of 422.0 thousand yen per year in the DSA (see Fig. 6.3). When examined by prefecture, it was found that social welfare increased in several prefectures, regardless of whether it was per capita.

   Second, as shown in the left-hand panel of Fig. 6.4, since decreases in real GDP were estimated as 1244 billion per year in total and JPY 1, 201 billion per year in the DSA, a marked decline in real GDP in the DSA was found (see Fig. 6.4). However, there was a slight increase in the real GDP in western Japan, and it was considered that interregional substitution in the production function in this study affected these results.

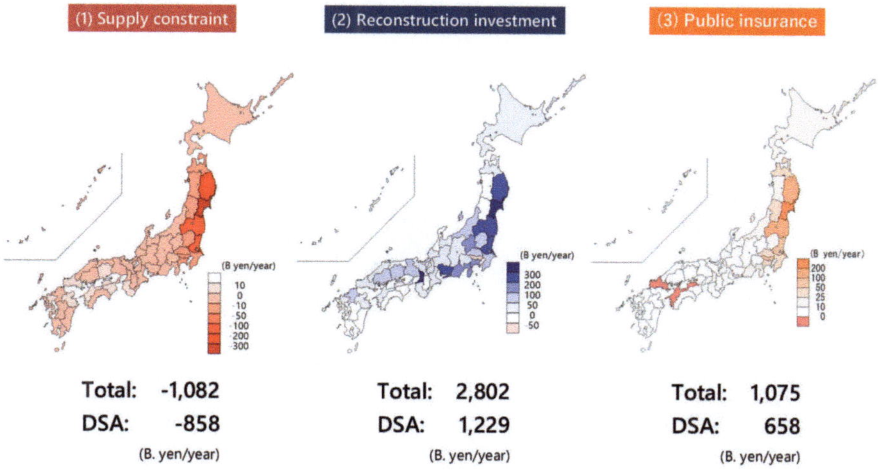

Fig. 6.2 Equivalent variation for each scenario and prefecture (Unit: billion yen/year)

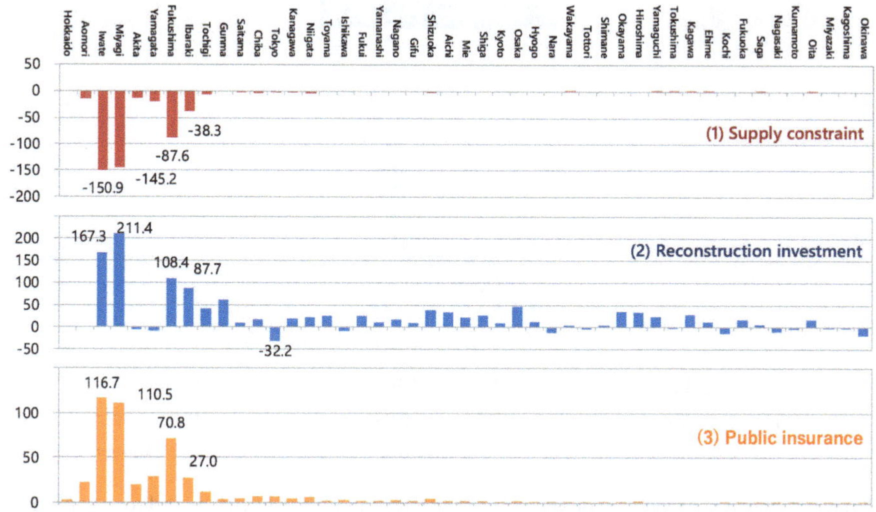

Fig. 6.3 Equivalent variation per capita for each scenario and prefecture (Unit: thousand yen/year)

Third, as shown in the left-hand panel of Fig. 6.5, decreases in prefectural production outputs were estimated at 2139 billion yen per year in total and 2024 billion yen per year in the DSA (see Fig. 6.5). These changes indicate a decrease in output of 0.23% per year in total and 3.22% per year in the DSA. Muto et al. (2012) estimated a decrease in the total output of 0.45% and 7.44% in the DSA. The changes in production output by industrial sector by prefecture, shown in the left-hand panel of Fig. 6.6, show that output fell in all industrial sectors in

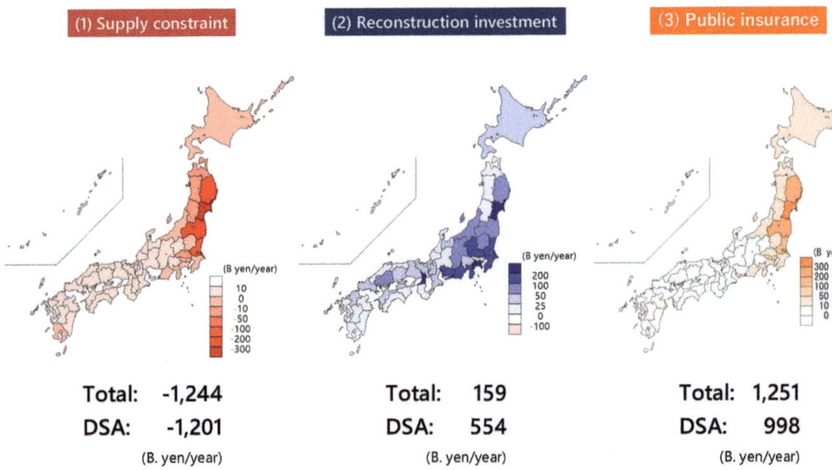

Fig. 6.4 Change in GDP for each scenario and prefecture (Unit: billion yen/year)

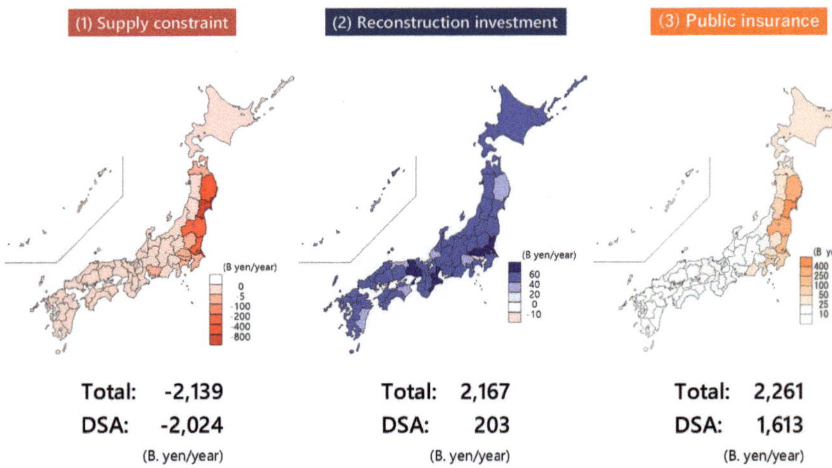

Fig. 6.5 Change in production output for each scenario and prefecture (Unit: billion yen/year)

the DSA as well as in the food sector (FOD) and construction sector (CNS) in the areas surrounding the DSA (see Fig. 6.6).

2. ***Regional Redistribution by Reconstruction Investment***

First, the middle panel of Fig. 6.2 shows that welfare improvements through reconstruction investment were estimated to be 2802 billion yen per year in total and 1229 billion yen per year in the DSA. In particular, welfare of JPY 500 billion per year improved in Miyagi. However, although welfare improved in some prefectures other than the DSA, it deteriorated significantly in Tokyo. In addition, as shown in the middle panel of Fig. 6.3, significant improvements in welfare per capita are achieved in the DSA. While the deterioration in welfare per capita in Tokyo was estimated as 32.2 thousand yen per year, the improvement

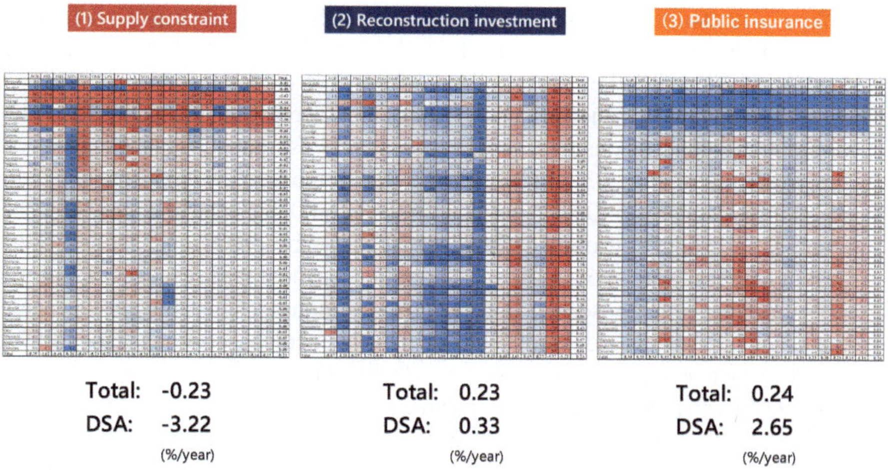

Fig. 6.6 Change rate of production output for each scenario, prefecture, and production sector (Unit: %/year)

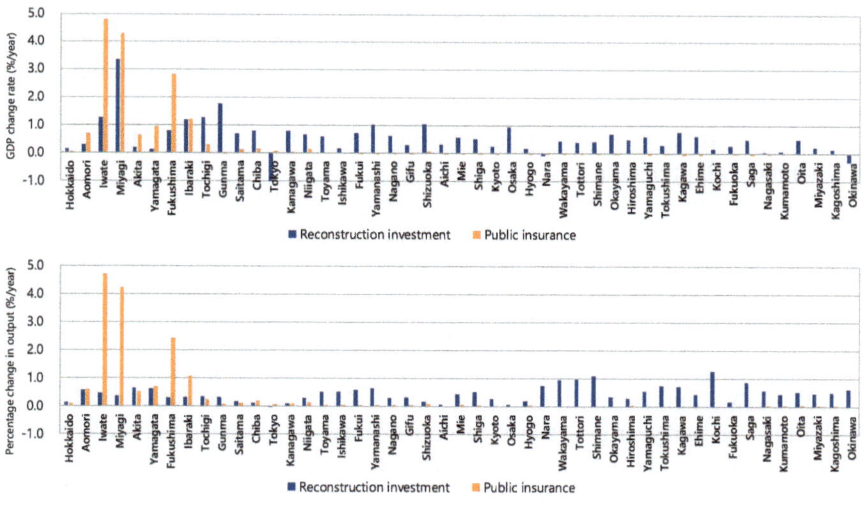

Fig. 6.7 Change rate of GDP and production output for each scenario and prefecture (Unit: %/year)

in welfare per capita in Miyagi was 211.4 thousand yen per year. Moreover, when examined by prefecture, social welfare decreases in several prefectures, except for Tokyo, regardless of whether it is per capita.

Second, as shown in the middle panel of Fig. 6.4, reconstruction investment contributed significantly to the improvement in real GDP in DSA, as the increase in real GDP was 159 billion yen per year in total and 554 billion yen per year in DSA. In particular, Miyagi, as shown in the top panel of Fig. 6.7, increased its real GDP by JPY 293 billion per year (see Fig. 6.7). However, although reconstruction investment increased the real GDP in most prefectures, the decrease in

Tokyo was estimated to be 2582 billion yen per year (3.0% per year). It is believed that the deterioration in Tokyo's real GDP resulted from the large amount of reconstruction funds collected from Tokyo's tax revenue.

Third, the middle panel of Fig. 6.5 shows that increases in prefectural production output due to reconstruction investment were estimated at 2167 billion yen per year in total and 203 billion yen per year in the DSA. These changes indicated improvements of 0.23% per year in total and 0.33% per year in DSA. The changes in production output by industrial sector by prefecture, shown in the middle panel of Fig. 6.6, show that the output of most industrial sectors in the DSA and that of many sectors in the secondary industries in prefectures, except the DSA, have recovered, while the output of the medical services sector (MED) and the other services sector (ANC) has declined nationally.

3. ***Income Compensation by Public Insurance***

First, as shown in the right-hand panel of Fig. 6.2, welfare improvement due to public insurance was estimated at 1075 billion yen per year in total and 658 billion yen per year in the DSA. In particular, welfare recovered in and around the DSA, but the farther away from the DSA, the smaller was the welfare improvement, with some prefectures (Yamaguchi, Kagawa, and Ehime) showing worsening welfare. In addition, the lower panel of Fig. 6.3 shows that welfare improvements per capita were estimated as 116.7 thousand yen per year in Iwate, 110.5 thousand yen per year in Miyagi, and a total of 324.9 thousand yen per year in the DSA. Nationally, the average per capita welfare improvement was estimated as 8.5 to yen per year, which means that per capita welfare improved in almost all prefectures.

Second, in the right-hand panel of Fig. 6.4, the change in real GDP due to public insurance increased by 1251 billion yen per year in total, and by 998 billion yen per year in the DSA, indicating that public insurance and reconstruction investment contributed significantly to the increase in real GDP in the DSA. The top panel of Fig. 6.7 shows that the estimated increase in real GDP was 251 billion yen per year (4.8% per year) in Iwate, 377 billion yen per year (4.3% per year) in Miyagi, 240 billion yen per year (2.8% per year) in Fukushima, and 130 billion yen per year (1.2% per year) in Ibaraki. In contrast, real GDP tends to decline in areas far from the DSA. However, in the case of public insurance, in contrast to reconstruction investment, Tokyo's real GDP increased by 51 billion yen per year (0.1% per year).

Third, the right-hand panel of Fig. 6.5 shows that the increase in prefectural production output due to public insurance was estimated at 2261 billion yen per year in total and 1613 billion yen per year in the DSA. These changes in production output represented a recovery of 0.24% per year for the national total and 2.65% per year for DSA, indicating that public insurance contributed significantly to the increase in production output in DSA. In addition, as shown in the bottom panel of Fig. 6.6, public insurance restored the production output of all industries in the DSA, as well as most industries in the prefectures surrounding the DSA. However, the output of secondary industries tended to decline in areas far from the DSA.

4. ***Discussion***

The results of our simulation analysis are as follows: First, we confirm the existence of asymmetric spillover effects of natural disasters, because changes in social welfare, real GDP, and production output due to the Great East Japan Earthquake varied across regions, sometimes taking both positive and negative values. Second, we confirm the existence of asymmetric spillover effects with respect to reconstruction investment. As one moves away from the DSA, the effect of reconstruction investment diminishes and can take both negative and positive values. Third, both reconstruction investment and public insurance restored social welfare, real GDP, and production output in the DSA under post-disaster conditions. The improvements in real GDP and production output from reconstruction investment are smaller than those from public insurance; however, the improvements in social welfare from reconstruction investment are larger than those from public insurance. However, reconstruction investment causes a large loss to Tokyo for all indicators. This is because Tokyo, which has the highest tax revenue, bears a higher share of expenditure on reconstruction investment, since it is assumed that 1 percent of the tax revenue is collected from each prefecture as a source of reconstruction revenue. Substituting $\alpha = 1$ into (7.25), we can confirm the change in ex post utility due to reconstruction investment. Accordingly, it is considered that ex post utility in Tokyo decreases because the proportion of the fiscal burden is higher than the ex post income improvement. On the other hand, public insurance provides smaller improvements for areas more distant from the DSA but improves social welfare while significantly improving GDP and output nationwide. Therefore, it is important to provide income compensation through public insurance as part of the post-disaster policy. Both policies achieved economic recovery from disasters, but the degree of recovery with asymmetric spillover effects differed significantly across regions. It is necessary to establish a risk-sharing system based on these effects, both ex post and ex ante.

6.4 Conclusion

This study theoretically examines a fiscal system for interregional risk sharing against natural disasters and measures the effects of post-earthquake reconstruction investment and income compensation, as well as the damage caused by the Great East Japan Earthquake, through quantitative analysis using an SCGE model. This study focuses on the asymmetric spillover effects of natural disasters and the related investments in disaster prevention, recovery, and reconstruction. Even if they occur locally, their effects can spread both nationally and asymmetrically through market transactions. This makes it difficult to allocate not only the ex ante costs of interregional risk sharing for natural disasters but also the ex post costs of recovery investments across regions. Therefore, this study examines not only investments in disaster prevention, recovery, and reconstruction but also income compensation through public insurance as an interregional risk-sharing instrument.

In the theoretical analysis of the ex ante case, after defining the asymmetric spillover effects of investment in disaster prevention, recovery, and reconstruction, as well as natural disasters, we examined the effects of interregional risk sharing by adding public insurance to investment in disaster prevention, recovery, and reconstruction. To increase the expected utility from investment in disaster prevention, recovery, and reconstruction, the marginal increase in income from investment in disaster prevention, recovery, and reconstruction must exceed the cost-burden ratio for that investment. This theoretical relationship suggests that it is difficult to reach an interregional consensus on investment in disaster prevention, recovery, and reconstruction, as some regions experience a decrease in income due to investment in recovery and reconstruction, as confirmed by quantitative analysis. On the other hand, for public insurance, as long as fair premiums are set, even in regions where income increases due to natural disasters, if the burden of investment in recovery and reconstruction is greater than the increase in income, purchasing insurance increases the expected utility in each region. This implies that with public insurance, the cost of recovery and reconstruction investment can be covered by the burden on regions whose income increases due to natural disasters. Furthermore, under the assumption of interregional risk sharing, where the central government encourages each region to voluntarily invest in disaster prevention, recovery, and reconstruction through subsidy policies and compensates for income through public insurance, we derive the conditions for a decentralized Nash equilibrium with local governments to become socially optimal. We also confirm that public insurance is necessary to guarantee the optimality of the Nash equilibrium, and in this sense, public insurance is complementary to investments in disaster prevention and recovery and reconstruction.

In the quantitative analysis of the ex post case, an SCGE analysis of the Great East Japan Earthquake confirmed the existence of the asymmetric spillover effects assumed in the theoretical analysis. Moreover, the results were consistent with the theoretical analysis, which showed that the expected utility decreased significantly in regions where the cost burden of reconstruction investment was large. In addition, since income compensation by public insurance improves ex post utility, real GDP, and output without significantly reducing ex post utility in a given region, as reconstruction investment does, the existence of public insurance is also confirmed to be important ex post.

However, income compensation through public insurance must be financed by subsidies considered in the ex ante case. Although financing through public bonds is an alternative method, there is also a method by which the government collects insurance premiums with a lump-sum tax added and accumulates them. From the perspective of fiscal consolidation, the latter method is preferable based on the fiscal system for interregional risk sharing and its effects identified in this chapter; however, it requires further study through dynamic analysis.

The remaining issues in this study are as follows: First, it would be interesting to introduce public goods that directly affect utility into theoretical analysis. Some public goods damaged by natural disasters directly affect utility, such as public goods used in tourism. Such public goods have been analyzed by Ihori (1999), but their interaction with the production-affecting public goods introduced in this chapter is unclear; therefore, there is room for theoretical investigation. Another issue to address is the introduction of population mobility, as discussed by Mansoorian (2000). In the quantitative analysis, it should be noted that although reconstruction investment and public insurance have been quite effective in both the DSA and all prefectures, we do not know how long it will take to progress toward and complete economic recovery from the disaster. Therefore, we need to use a forward-looking dynamic model or a recursive dynamic model for analysis.

References

Ban, K., (2007) "Development of a multiregional dynamic applied general equilibrium model for the Japanese economy: regional economic analysis based on a forward-looking perspective," *RIETI Discussion Paper Series*, 07-J-043, pp 1–52 (in Japanese).

Cabinet Office, Government of Japan (2011a), *Getsurei-keizai-houkoku-tou Ni Kansuru Kankei-kakuryo-kaigi Shinsai-taiou-tokubetsu-kaigou-siryo: Tohoku-chihou Taiheiyou-Oki Jishin No Macro-Keizaiteki-eikyou No Bunseki* (English title unavailable), March 23.

Cabinet Office, Government of Japan (2011b), *Higashi-nihon-daishinsai Ni Okeru Higai-gaku No Suikei Ni Tsuite* (English title unavailable), June 24.

Development Bank of Japan (2011a), "Higashi-nihon-daishinsai Shihon Stock Higai-kingaku-suikei Ni Tsuite: Area-betsu (Kenbetu/Nairiku-enganbetsu) Ni Suitei," (English title unavailable). *DBJ News*, April 28.

Development Bank of Japan (2011b), "Higashi-nihon-daishinsai Shihon Stock Higai-kingaku-suikei Ni Tsuite: Area-betsu (Kenbetu/Nairiku-enganbetsu) Ni Suitei ,"(English title unavailable), *DBJ News*, July 21.

Hayashiyama, Y., M. Abe and N. Sakamoto (2012) "Measuring macro-economic damage of the Great East Japan earth-quake using the multi-region and multi-sector CGE model," *Policy Management Studies*, Faculty of Policy Management, Tohoku Bunka Gakuen University, 1(11):159–190. (in Japanese).

Hosoe, N., K. Gasawa and H. Hashimoto (2010) *Textbook of Computable General Equilibrium Modelling: Programming and Simulations*, Palgrave, Macmillan.

Ihori, T. (1992) "Impure public goods and transfers in a three agent model," *Journal of Public Economics*, 48, 385–401.

Ihori, T. (1999) "An economic analysis of public transfers," *Japanese Economic Review*, 50(1), 44–60.

Ishikawa, Y. and T. Miyagi (2004) "An interregional industrial linkage analysis in Japan: using a 47-regional interregional input-output table," *Studies in Regional Science*, 34(1), 139–152 (in Japanese).

Mansoorian, A. (2000) "Risk sharing in a federation with population mobility and long horizons," *Canadian Journal of Economics*, 33(3), 662–676.

Mansoorian, A. and G. M. Myers (1993) "Attachment to home and efficient purchases of population in a fiscal externality economy," *Journal of Public Economics*, 52, 117–132.

Miyagi, T., Y. Ishikawa, S. Yuri and K. Tsuchiya (2003) "The construction of interregional input-output table at prefecture level using intraregional input-output tables," *Infrastructure Planning Review*, 20(1), 87–95 (in Japanese).

Muto, S., M. Aoki, H. Morisugi, T. Kamiizumi and S. Kirikoshi (2012) "SCGE Model Ni Yoru Higashi-nihon-daishinsai No Macro-Keizaiteki-higai-keisoku," (English title unavailable), *Proceedings of infrastructure and planning*, CD-ROM, Japan Society of Civil Engineers 45, 1–16 (in Japanese).

Myers, G. M. (1990) "Optimality, free mobility, and the regional authority in a federation," *Journal of Public Economics*, 63, 107–121.

Nakajima, K. and N. Sakamoto (2015) "General equilibrium analysis of regional redistributive effects of investment for reconstruction from the Great East Japan Earthquake," *Proceedings of the 55th European Congress of Regional Science Association International*, Paper No. 00320, pp. 1–36.

Persson, T. and G. Tabellini (1996a) "Federal fiscal constitutions: Risk sharing and moral hazard," *Econometrica*, 64(3), 623–646.

Persson, T. and G. Tabellini (1996b) "Federal fiscal constitutions: risk sharing and redistribution," *Journal of Political Economy*, 104(5), 979–1009.

Shibata, H. (1971) "A bargaining model of the pure theory of public expenditures," *Journal of Political Economy*, 79(1), 1–29.

Warr, P. G. (1983) "The private provision of a public good is independent of the distribution of income," *Economics Letters*, 13, 207–211.

MIX
Papier aus verantwortungsvollen Quellen
Paper from responsible sources
FSC® C105338

If you have any concerns about our products,
you can contact us on
ProductSafety@springernature.com

In case Publisher is established outside the EU,
the EU authorized representative is:
Springer Nature Customer Service Center GmbH
Europaplatz 3, 69115 Heidelberg, Germany

Printed by Libri Plureos GmbH
in Hamburg, Germany